Modern Caribbean Cuisine

Modern Caribbean Cuisine

Wendy Rahamut

Interlink Books

An imprint of Interlink Publishing Group, Inc.
Northampton, Massachusetts

First published in 2007 by

Interlink Books
An imprint of Interlink Publishing Group, Inc.
46 Crosby Street, Northampton, Massachusetts 01060
www.interlinkbooks.com

Library of Congress Cataloging-in-Publication Data available

HB ISBN-10: 1-56656-653-3
HB ISBN-13: 978-156656-653-7
PB ISBN-10: 1-56656-676-2
PB ISBN-13: 978-1-56656-676-6

Food styling by Wendy Rahamut
Book design by IKON Design
Photography by Michael Bonaparte
Map by Peter Harper

Printed and bound in Thailand

To request our complete 40-page full-color catalog, please call us toll
free at **1-800-238-LINK**, visit our website at www.interlinkbooks.com,
or send us an e-mail: **info@interlinkbooks.com**

Contents

introduction

The Caribbean islands boast some of the most beautiful landscapes in the world, the friendliest of peoples and the most colorful of cuisines. Our deep turquoise blue waters provide us with a vast assortment of fresh seafood on a daily basis, the rich soil in some of our tropical rainforested countries gives us all our fresh vegetables and herbs, and our delicious and intriguing ground or root provisions. Our tropical fruits, delightfully juicy and sugary sweet, can be likened to the splendor of a Caribbean sunset with their vibrant hues of brilliant yellow and orange. Our sugar cane is rated the best in the world for both white and brown sugar and our rums are always placed top of the ratings. We are indeed a richly endowed set of islands and thereby largely self-sufficient in agriculture. The longer I live in the Caribbean, the more amazed I become not only at the deliciousness of our local ingredients and food, but at the versatility of our indigenous ingredients.

Traditional Caribbean food has gained the reputation for being a little heavy and high in fat content, though very tasty all the same! It is a cuisine historically comprised of rich brown stews, rice and pea dishes sometimes simmered in coconut milk, provisions and starches enveloped in sauces, spicy curries and rotis, vegetables cooked with butter, flaky pastries, tender mouth-watering breads and, of course, butter cakes and creamy desserts.

These represent a rich inheritance from our African, Indian and European ancestors respectively. They are all foods infused with our own locally grown fresh herbs and embellished with each island's own version of pepper sauce or salsa made from fresh hot peppers and fruits.

Globalization has made our world a smaller place to live in, with influences from everywhere touching our lives with respect to music, culture and, of course, food. The challenge then becomes both to maintain our own integrity and to integrate other influences as well into our cooking. This is what *Modern Caribbean Cuisine* is all about.

There are some traditional recipes within these pages, but the main emphasis of this book is about embracing our own indigenous ingredients and using them in such a way as to create a fresher, tastier, spicy and delicious cuisine – a true celebration of Caribbean flavors as they are today. The dishes use fresh foods, enhanced with our own blend of herbs, spiced up with our local peppers and infused with our dried spices. They all come together to make a Caribbean fusion cuisine that is, in the best sense, addictive!

Conversion Tables

Weights

1 ounce	30 grams
8 ounces or ½ pound	250 grams or ¼ kilogram
16 ounces or 1 pound	500 grams or ½ kilogram

Volumes

1 teaspoon	5 ml
1 tablespoon	15 ml
½ cup	125 ml
1 cup	250 ml or ½ pint
2 cups	500 ml or 1 pint

Oven Temperatures

250ºF = 120ºC

300ºF = 150ºC

350ºF = 180ºC

400ºF = 200ºC

The Bahamas

Turks and
Caicos Islands

Dominican
Republic

Haiti

Cuba

Cayman
Islands

Jamaica

Mexico

Virgin Is.

Anguilla

St Martin

Barbuda

Antigua

Montserrat

Guadeloupe

Dominica

Martinique

St Lucia

St Vincent

Barbados

Grenada

Tobago

Trinidad

Puerto
Rico

St Kitts and Nevis

Atlantic Ocean

Caribbean Sea

N

km

miles

0   150   300   450   600   750

0   100   200   300   400   500

3

snacks & appetizers

Caribbean people love to enjoy a good party or 'lime' (informal gathering), and always present are drinks and, of course, food.

On the islands, formal plated appetizers or hors d'oeuvres are not very popular, though you'll find them at smart dinner parties and fine dining restaurants. However, there are no boundaries where light tasty snack foods are concerned! This section gives you some of those portable and delightful snacks that you would encounter on a visit to any of the islands, each contributing its own distinct flavor. Some of the recipes here would traditionally be fried but I've adjusted them to allow for baked versions as well. There are lots of delicious seafood snacks and elegant appetizers, such as shrimp cocktail, smoked herring dip, shrimp pâté and a savory sponge roll with shrimp filling. There are also great cutters (tapas) to enjoy while on a 'lime', like fish fritters, Mexican empanadas, Jamaican beef patties, conch fritters and conch souse, just to name a few. All are distinctly Caribbean, infused with hot peppers and flavored with our aromatic and indigenous fresh herbs.

Mexican Empanadas

Mexican empanadas are traditionally fried pies.
This version is baked, which gives a delicious pie with longer staying
power! Serve as a light snack or as an appetizer.

FOR THE DOUGH

- **4 cups flour**
- **2 tsp paprika**
- **1 tsp salt**
- **1 cup shortening**
- **½ cup water**

FOR THE FILLING

- **2 tbs vegetable oil**
- **1 cup chopped fresh herbs**
- **2 garlic cloves, chopped**
- **2 pimento peppers,
  seeded and chopped**
- **½ hot pepper, chopped**
- **1 onion, chopped**
- **1 lb ground chicken or beef**
- **½ cup raisins**
- **⅓ cup sliced green olives**
- **1 egg, beaten**

- To make the dough: combine the flour with the paprika and salt. Cut in the shortening until it's the size of small peas. Add the water and bring the mixture together. Refrigerate until ready for use.
- Preheat oven to 400°F.
- Heat the oil in a frying pan, and add the chopped herbs, garlic, peppers and onion. Sauté until tender, about 4 minutes, then add the meat and cook until no longer pink, about 5 minutes. If the meat seems lumpy, put it into a food processor bowl and process for 30 seconds, just until fine.
- Remove from the heat and add the raisins and olives. Season with salt and freshly ground black pepper. Divide the dough into 20 equal pieces and roll each piece of dough into a 4 inch circle. Place about 1 tablespoon of filling in the center of the lower half. Fold over and seal, using a little water if necessary.
- Place on a greased baking sheet and brush with beaten egg. Repeat until all the dough and filling are used up.
- Bake for 20–25 minutes until golden. Serve with spicy tomato salsa (page 311).

Makes 20

Conch Souse

Souse is enjoyed all through the Caribbean
and can be likened to a seviche. Lots of lip-puckering fresh lime
juice is used, along with hot peppers and fresh herbs.
Pigs' feet are traditionally soused, as are
chicken feet. I love this version made with conch or lambie.
It can be served in small glasses as an appetizer.

- **2 lb conch,
  cleaned, tenderized and
  chopped (see page 63)**
- **1 onion, chopped**
- **1 cucumber, chopped**
- **juice of 2 large limes**
- **½ cup chopped parsley**
- **¼ cup chopped cilantro
  (chadon beni)**
- **1 hot pepper, seeded and chopped**
- **1 lime, sliced**
- **salt and freshly ground
  black pepper**

- Steam the conch for
about 3–4 minutes, then remove
from the steamer and drain.
- Place in a glass bowl, add the rest
of the ingredients and cover and
refrigerate for about 3–4 hours.
- Serve cold.

Serves 4–6

Breadfruit Pies

- **2 lb breadfruit, peeled and cut into quarters**
- **1 tsp salt**
- **¼ cup melted butter**
- **¾ cup flour**
- **2 tbs vegetable oil**
- **2 garlic cloves, minced**
- **1 small onion, minced**
- **½ carrot, finely chopped**
- **½ cup finely chopped fresh herbs**
- **½ lb ground chicken**
- **⅓ cup chopped parsley**
- **1 egg, beaten**
- **1 cup fine toasted bread crumbs**

● Boil the breadfruit with the salt in plenty of water until tender, about 20–30 minutes. While still hot, crush the breadfruit and add the melted butter and ¼ cup of flour. Combine until the mixture starts to stay together. Knead for a few minutes, cover and set aside.

● Heat the oil in a sauté pan and add the garlic and onion. Sauté for a few minutes, then add the carrot and mixed fresh herbs. Add the ground chicken and cook until tender. Season with salt and freshly ground black pepper. Cook for about 15 minutes, remove from the heat, add the parsley and leave mixture to cool.

● Preheat oven to 375ºF.

● Flour a work surface and roll out breadfruit dough to about ¼ inch thickness. Stamp out circles with a 3 inch cutter.

● Place about 1 tablespoon of filling on the lower portion of each circle. Fold over, and seal with a fork. Dust with the remaining flour, brush with beaten egg and roll in bread crumbs.

● Bake for about 15 minutes until golden.

Makes about 10

Jamaican Beef Patties

- 1 egg, beaten

FOR THE PASTRY
- 3 cups all-purpose flour
- 1 tsp salt
- 1 tsp baking powder
- 1 cup vegetable shortening
- a few drops of yellow food coloring or annatto oil
- 1 cup ice water

FOR THE FILLING
- 2 tbs vegetable oil
- 2 garlic cloves, minced
- 1 onion, finely chopped
- 1 lb ground beef
- 1 large sprig of French thyme
- ½ cup chopped chives
- 2 hot pepper, seeded and chopped
- ¼ tsp allspice powder
- 1 tsp sugar
- 2 tbs tomato paste
- 2 cups bread crumbs

- To make the pastry: place all the dried ingredients into a bowl. Cut the shortening into ½ inch pieces and add to the flour, breaking the shortening into tiny pieces the size of small peas or bread crumbs.
- Add the coloring to the water, then add just enough water to the mixture to bring the pastry together with your hands. Form it into a ball, divide in half, then wrap in plastic and refrigerate until ready for use.

- To make the filling: heat the oil in a sauté pan with a lid. Add the garlic and onion and cook until fragrant. Add the beef and stir. Add the thyme, chives, hot pepper, allspice, sugar, and salt to taste.
- Stir in the tomato paste and cook until the meat is brown in color. Cover and simmer for about 15 minutes, adding a little water to prevent sticking. Stir in the bread crumbs and adjust seasoning to taste.
- Leave to cool.
- Preheat oven to 400°F.
- Roll out the pastry to about ¼ inch thickness and stamp out circles about 4 inches in diameter.
- Place about 2 teaspoons of the filling on the lower half of each pastry circle. Fold top over bottom to form a half moon. Seal with a fork. Brush with beaten egg. Repeat until all the pastry and filling is used up.
- Place the patties on a baking sheet and bake for about 15–20 minutes until golden brown.

Makes about 25

For a lighter dish
Use ground chicken.

Shrimp & Mushroom Thermidor with Parsley & Parmesan Gratin

A traditional French appetizer that has made a comeback.

- **2 lb fresh medium white shrimp, peeled and deveined**
- **2 garlic cloves, minced**
- **½ tsp salt**
- **1 cup mushrooms, cleaned and sliced**

FOR THE SAUCE
- **3 tbs unsalted butter**
- **3 tbs all-purpose flour**
- **1 cup milk**
- **2 egg yolks**
- **½ cup white wine**
- **½ cup grated Parmesan cheese**
- **½ tsp cayenne pepper**
- **½ tsp powdered mustard**

FOR THE GRATIN
- **½ cup dry bread crumbs**
- **2 tbs butter**
- **2 tbs chopped parsley**
- **2 tbs grated Parmesan cheese**
- **salt and freshly ground black pepper**

- Combine the shrimp with the garlic and salt and set aside.
- To make the sauce: melt the butter in a heavy medium-sized saucepan, stir in the flour and cook until smooth and almost liquid. Add the milk and cook, stirring well until the mixture thickens.
- Add the shrimp and mushrooms, cover, and simmer for 5 minutes. Remove from the heat and add the egg yolks and wine. Stir to combine.
- Place on a low heat to warm the mixture only. Do not boil or else the eggs will curdle. Add the Parmesan cheese, cayenne pepper and mustard.
- Preheat broiler or grill.
- Spoon the shrimp mixture into buttered Thermidor dishes or shallow ramekins.
- Combine all the ingredients for the gratin. Sprinkle on top of the shrimp and place under broiler until golden on top.

Serves 4–6

For a lighter dish
Omit the eggs and use skim milk.

Spicy Tobago Crab Fritters with Cocktail Sauce

- **2 x 4 oz cans crab meat, drained**
- **1 medium potato, boiled and crushed**
- **2 eggs, lightly beaten**
- **2 tbs softened butter**
- **1 pimento pepper, seeded and chopped**
- **2 tbs chopped chives**
- **3 tbs chopped cilantro (chadon beni)**
- **2 tbs chopped parsley**
- **2 garlic cloves, minced**
- **2 tbs fresh lime juice**
- **1 tsp pepper sauce**
- **1 cup soft bread crumbs**
- **1 cup flour**
- **vegetable oil for frying**

- Place the crab in a large mixing bowl. Remove any cartilage and add the potato, half the beaten egg, the softened butter, pepper, herbs, garlic, lime juice and pepper sauce. Combine well.
- Add enough bread crumbs to hold the mixture together.
- Form the mixture into 2 inch patties, dip in the remaining egg and then in the flour to coat evenly.
- Heat some oil in a frying pan or wok. Fry the fritters until golden brown, drain, and serve hot with cocktail dipping sauce.

Makes about 12–15

Cocktail Sauce

- **1 cup tomato ketchup**
- **¼ cup fresh lime juice**
- **¼ cup mayonnaise**
- **2 tbs horseradish sauce**
- **1 tsp pepper sauce**

- Combine all the ingredients. Stir together, then add salt to taste.

Makes 1 cup

For a lighter dish
Brush the patties with vegetable oil and bake in a preheated oven at 375ºF for 20 minutes until golden brown.

Caribbean Fish Balls
with Pink Sauce

- **1 lb boneless fresh fish, cubed**
- **½ cup cornstarch**
- **¼ cup chopped chives**
- **¼ cup chopped basil**
- **½ tsp cayenne pepper**
- **1 tbs fresh lime juice**
- **vegetable oil for frying**

● Place the fish, ¼ cup cornstarch, the chives, basil, cayenne, lime juice and salt and freshly ground black pepper into a food processor and process to a paste.
● Put the rest of the cornstarch on a plate. Form the fish paste into small balls about 1 inch in diameter, and dredge in the cornstarch.
● Heat some oil in a frying pan or wok and fry the fish balls until golden. Drain on paper towels.

Makes 15–20

Pink Sauce

- **½ cup low fat mayonnaise**
- **½ cup plain yogurt**
- **2 tbs horseradish sauce**
- **1 garlic clove, minced**
- **¼ cup finely chopped cilantro (chadon beni)**
- **2 tbs tomato ketchup**

● To make the dip, combine all the ingredients except the ketchup. Mix in the ketchup, taste and adjust seasonings.

Makes about 1 cup

Bene-crusted Shrimp Balls

Bene seeds are much liked in the Caribbean, where we make bene squares and bene balls – both popular candies. They are quite similar to sesame seeds, so you can easily make the substitution. Serve the shrimp balls with plum sauce.

- 1 lb shrimp, peeled and deveined
- 2 tbs cornstarch
- 1 tbs soy sauce
- 2 tbs minced chives
- 2 garlic cloves, minced
- 1 inch piece of ginger
- ½ tsp sesame oil
- ½ cup water chestnuts
- ½ cup flour
- ½ tsp white pepper
- 1 egg, beaten
- ½ cup bene or sesame seeds
- vegetable oil for deep frying

- In a food processor combine the shrimp, cornstarch, soy sauce, chives, garlic, ginger, sesame oil, and salt and pepper to taste. Process to a smooth texture, then add the chestnuts and process just until they are chopped. Taste the mixture and adjust seasoning.
- Form the shrimp mixture into 1 inch balls.
- Mix the flour and pepper. Dredge the shrimp balls in flour, then dip in the egg and roll in the bene or sesame seeds to coat.
- Deep fry until golden.

Makes about 15–20

Tip
Deep frying these appetizers works better for all-around browning of the shrimp balls.

French Onion Tartlets

This is a French Caribbean speciality

FOR THE PASTRY
- **2 cups all-purpose flour**
- **pinch of salt**
- **1 tsp paprika**
- **1 tsp dried oregano**
- **1 cup unsalted butter**
- **⅓ cup ice cold water**

FOR THE FILLING
- **4 tbs olive oil**
- **3 lb onions, peeled and sliced**
- **¼ cup French thyme**
- **2 tbs evaporated milk**
- **1 cup grated Parmesan cheese**

• To make the pastry: put the flour, salt, paprika, oregano and butter into the bowl of a food processor and process for 10 seconds until the mixture resembles fine bread crumbs. Add the water and combine.

• Remove from the processor and bring the dough together with your hands. Refrigerate for 15 minutes.

• Roll out the dough to about ¼ inch thickness and stamp out 3 inch circles. Place on a lined baking sheet and refrigerate.

• Preheat oven to 400ºF.

• To make the filling: heat the olive oil in a sauté pan, add the onions, and cook until tender on a low heat for about 20–25 minutes, stirring often.

• Add the thyme and cook for a few minutes more. Stir in the evaporated milk and cook until creamy. Season with salt and freshly ground black pepper, remove from the heat and leave to cool.

• Spoon the cooled filling onto the pastry rounds and bake for 15 minutes. Sprinkle with the Parmesan and bake for 5 minutes more.

Makes 24

19

Crispy Cornmeal &
Chili Coated Wings with
Cilantro Dip

- 3 lb chicken wings (about 20 wings)
- 2 tbs minced chives
- 1 tbs minced garlic
- 1 tbs olive oil
- 1 cup flour
- 1 cup yellow cornmeal
- 1 tbs ground roasted cumin (geera)
- 1 tsp salt
- 2 tsp black pepper
- 2 tsp chili powder
- 2 eggs

FOR THE DIP
- 1½ cups sour cream
- ½ cup mayonnaise
- 1 cup chopped cilantro
  (chadon beni)
- ½ cup chopped chives
- 1 hot pepper, seeded and chopped
- salt to taste

- Preheat oven to 375ºF.
- Discard the wing tips and cut the chicken wings in half. Pat dry with paper towels. Mix the minced chives with the garlic and olive oil, and rub the mixture over the wings.
- In a flat dish, combine the flour with the cornmeal, cumin, salt, pepper and chili powder.
- Beat the eggs in another flat dish.
- Dip the halved chicken wings first into the flour mixture, then into the beaten eggs, then again into the flour.
- Place on an oiled baking sheet and bake for 20 minutes. Turn, and continue baking for 30 minutes.
- Combine all the ingredients for the dip.
- Serve the crispy wings on a platter with the dip.

Makes about 40

Coo Coo Strips

Coo coo in the Caribbean is similar to Italian polenta.
Here, we toss in some flavoring agents and often add
ochroes as well. Some islands also add coconut milk.
In this version I have omitted the ochroes and the result
makes a delicious appetizer!

- **6 cups chicken stock or water**
- **2 pimento peppers,
  seeded and chopped**
- **2 garlic cloves, minced**
- **3 cups yellow cornmeal**
- **½ cup grated Parmesan cheese**
- **1 cup flour**
- **1 tsp paprika**
- **vegetable oil for frying**

- Boil the stock or water in a large saucepan and add the peppers, garlic, and salt and freshly ground black pepper.
- Pour in the cornmeal, whisking vigorously to prevent lumping, stir well and cook until the mixture becomes stiff and smooth and moves away from the sides of the pan.
- Generously butter a shallow cake pan or baking tray. Spread the mixture smoothly onto the tray, so that it is about 1 inch thick. Chill until very stiff.
- Combine the flour, paprika and some salt and pepper.
- Cut the polenta into strips, 2 inches x 1 inch.
- Coat the strips in the flour mixture and fry in hot oil until golden.
- Drain and serve immediately with spicy tomato salsa (page 311).

Serves 6–8

Arepa Coins
with Creamy Crab

- ½ cup butter
- 2 cups yellow cornmeal
- ½ cup grated cheese
- ½ cup chopped chives
- 2 tsp salt
- 2 cups hot water
- vegetable oil for frying

• Combine the butter and cornmeal and rub into the flour. Mix in the cheese, chives and salt. Add the hot water and knead to a soft dough.
• Roll to ½ inch thickness and stamp out 1½ inch diameter pieces.
• Heat the oil in a frying pan and shallow fry until golden and cooked, about 5 minutes.
• Drain and serve spread with your choice of topping, such as salsa, spicy shrimp or creamy crab.

Makes 32

Creamy Crab

- 1 cup crab meat, picked over
- ⅓ cup mayonnaise
- ½ tsp pepper sauce
- 1 tsp fresh lime juice
- salt to taste
- ¼ cup finely chopped fresh herbs (cilantro, chives, parsley)

• Combine all the ingredients. Spoon onto the arepa coins and serve immediately.

Makes about 1½ cups

For a lighter dish
Use low fat mayonnaise.

Shrimp Accras
of Martinique

Accras are traditionally French Caribbean in origin and
are usually made with salted cod.
This version uses shrimp, which gives a delicious new twist!

- **1 lb shrimp, cleaned**
- **½ cup flour**
- **1 tsp baking powder**
- **1 hot pepper, seeded and chopped**
- **½ cup chopped chives**
- **1 small onion, chopped**
- **1 tsp minced garlic**
- **2 tbs thyme**
- **½ tsp salt**
- **vegetable oil for frying**

- Heat a large non-stick frying pan, add the shrimp and dry roast on the pan. Turn and cook until the shrimp are pink and curled.
- Remove shrimp from pan and chop finely.
- Combine with the flour, baking powder, hot pepper, chives, onion, garlic, thyme and salt. Add enough water (about ½ cup) to make a soft batter-like dough.
- Heat the oil. Drop the batter by spoonfuls into the hot oil and fry until golden brown and puffed.
- Serve with green mango and thyme chutney (page 312).

Makes 15–20

Savory Sponge Roll with Shrimp Filling

FOR THE SPONGE
- ¼ cup butter
- ½ cup all-purpose flour
- 2 cups milk
- 4 eggs, separated

FOR THE FILLING
- 1 lb fresh shrimp, steamed and finely chopped
- ½ cup sour cream or thick plain yogurt
- 2 tbs finely chopped parsley
- ½ cup mayonnaise
- 1 tsp pepper sauce
- 2 tbs chopped chives
- 2 tbs fresh lime juice
- salt and freshly ground black pepper

- Preheat oven to 375°F.
- To make the sponge: line then grease and flour a 10 x 15 inch jellyroll pan or shallow baking tray.
- Melt the butter in a heavy saucepan, add the flour and stir until smooth. Add the milk and cook until smooth and thick.
- Beat the egg yolks. Add half to the milk mixture, stir, then add this to the remaining yolks.
- Beat the egg whites until peaks form and fold into the sauce. Pour into the prepared tin and bake for 12–15 minutes or until the sponge is golden and springs back when touched.

- Remove from the oven and invert onto a clean tea towel. Remove from pan and peel off the lining paper. Roll up, using the towel to help, and set aside until ready for use.
- To make the filling: combine all the ingredients, taste and adjust seasoning.
- Unroll the sponge and spread filling on top. Roll up jellyroll style. If you want a fuller roll start at the short end; if you want smaller slices, roll up from the long side.
- Wrap tightly in plastic and refrigerate for 1–2 hours.
- Remove and slice on the diagonal. Serve on a bed of fresh salad greens.

Makes 12 slices

For a lighter dish
Use low fat mayonnaise and sour cream or yogurt.

Baked Potato Pies

Traditional potato pies are fried and are a popular street food in Trinidad. This version is baked in a tender dough.

- 1 lb potatoes, peeled and cut into quarters
- ½ tbs vegetable oil
- 1 small onion, finely chopped
- ¼ cup finely chopped chives
- 2 tbs chopped cilantro (chadon beni)
- 2 garlic cloves, minced
- 1 pimento pepper, seeded and chopped
- ½ Congo pepper or hot pepper, seeded and chopped (optional)
- 2 tsp ground roasted cumin (geera)
- pepper sauce to taste
- 1 quantity pie dough (page 30)
- 1 egg, beaten

- Boil the potatoes with a little salt until tender. When cooked, drain and crush well with a potato masher.
- Heat the oil in a small frying pan. Add the onion, chives, cilantro, garlic and peppers. Fry for just 1 minute then pour into the mashed potato. Stir to combine. Add the cumin and pepper sauce, salt and freshly ground black pepper.
- Taste and adjust seasoning.
- Preheat oven to 375°F.
- Divide the dough into 24 equal pieces. Roll each piece into a 4 inch circle. Place about 1 tablespoon of filling in the center of the lower half. Fold over and seal, using a little water if necessary. Place on a greased baking sheet and brush with beaten egg.
- Bake for 15–20 minutes until lightly browned.

Makes 24

Shrimp Arepas with Spicy Tomato & Cheese

As you travel through the Spanish Caribbean the word 'arepas' means a fried cornmeal cake. In other parts it is more like a turnover, the pastry made from cornmeal, and stuffed with a spicy meat filling and fried.
This version is made with shrimp and can be baked or fried.

- **oil for brushing**

FOR THE PASTRY
- **2 cups cornmeal**
- **1 cup all-purpose flour**
- **3 tsp baking powder**
- **1 tsp brown sugar**
- **½ cup butter**

FOR THE FILLING
- **2 tbs vegetable oil**
- **4 garlic cloves, minced**
- **1 hot pepper, seeded and chopped**
- **1 small onion, chopped**
- **2 lb shrimp, cleaned and finely chopped**
- **1 cup chopped chives**
- **¼ cup French thyme**
- **½ cup tomato sauce (page 194)**
- **¼ cup cilantro (chadon beni)**
- **2 cups grated Cheddar cheese (optional)**

• To make the pastry: combine all the dry ingredients, then add the butter and rub into the mixture. Add enough warm water to make a soft dough. Divide into 16 pieces and cover with a wet tea towel.

• To make the filling: heat the oil in a sauté pan with a lid and add the garlic, pepper and onion. Cook until fragrant, add the shrimp and cook for a few seconds, then add the chives and thyme and cook for a few minutes more. Add the tomato sauce and season with salt. Cover and simmer for 10 minutes, then add the chopped cilantro and leave to cool.
• Preheat oven to 375ºF.
• Form the pieces of dough into balls. Press down on the balls to form 4–5 inch circles. Fill with the cooled shrimp mixture and sprinkle with cheese, if using.
• Fold into a half moon shape and place on a lined baking sheet. Brush the arepas with oil and bake for 20 minutes.
• Cool on a wire rack. Serve with spicy tomato salsa (page 311).

Makes 16

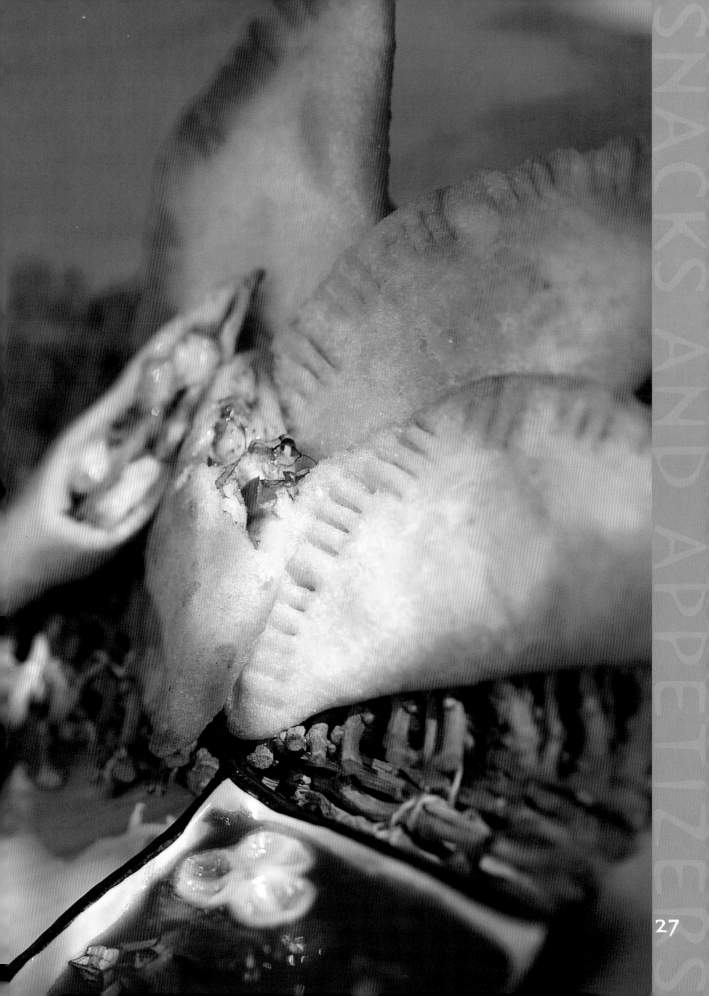

Spicy Smoked Herring Spread

Smoked and dried fish are popular on the islands. Here smoked herring flavors up a spicy spread for a truly exotic taste!

- **1 smoked herring fillet (about 1 oz)**
- **4 oz cream cheese**
- **⅓ cup mayonnaise**
- **1 tsp pepper sauce (or to taste)**
- **1 tsp fresh lime juice**
- **½ cup chopped fresh herbs (parsley, chives, basil)**

- Soak the herring in hot water for 20 minutes. Rinse, and pick out the bones.
- Place in a food processor and chop finely. Add the rest of the ingredients and process to a thick paste. Refrigerate until ready for use.
- Serve on crackers or toast rounds, sprinkled with additional herbs and garnished with sweet red pepper strips.

Makes about 1 cup

For a lighter dish
Use low fat mayonnaise and cream cheese.

Broccoli & Feta Pies

- **8 oz feta cheese or sharp Cheddar cheese**
- **1 lb broccoli, cut into ½ inch pieces**
- **½ tsp grated nutmeg**
- **½ cup soft bread crumbs**
- **½ batch pie dough (see right)**

- Combine the feta with the broccoli. Mix in the bread crumbs, then add the nutmeg and season with salt and freshly ground black pepper. Set aside.
- Preheat oven to 375ºF.
- Divide dough into 12 equal pieces. Roll each piece into a 4 inch circle and place about 1 tablespoon of filling in the center of the lower half. Fold over and seal, pinching the edges together, using a little water if necessary. Place on a greased baking sheet.
- Repeat until all dough and filling are used up.
- Bake for 15–20 minutes until lightly browned.

Makes 12

Pie Dough

- **4½ cups all-purpose flour**
- **1 package instant yeast (1 tablespoon)**
- **1 cup milk**
- **⅓ cup butter or margarine, melted**
- **⅓ cup sugar**
- **1 tsp salt**
- **2 eggs**

- In a mixer bowl combine 2 cups flour and the yeast.
- Heat the milk, butter, sugar and salt to 115–120ºF. Add to the flour mixture. Add the eggs and beat slowly until incorporated.
- Add as much of the remaining flour as you can, then turn onto a floured surface and knead for about 6–8 minutes to make a moderately stiff dough that is smooth and elastic.
- Place in a greased bowl, cover, and leave to rise until doubled in bulk (about 45 minutes).
- Punch down and let dough rest for 10 minutes before using.

Chow Mein Pies

Chow mein is a popular Chinese dish, and when made into pies and baked it makes a delicious meatless snack or light meal.

- **2 tbs low sodium soy sauce**
- **1 tsp sesame oil**
- **1 tbs sherry or rum (optional)**
- **1 tbs oyster sauce (optional)**
- **1 tsp Chinese chili sauce**
- **1 tsp cornstarch or potato flour**
- **1 tbs vegetable oil**
- **1 tbs ginger, shredded**
- **1 garlic clove, minced**
- **1 cup julienned carrots**
- **1 cup julienned chayotes**
- **1 cup shredded bok choy (pak choi)**
- **1 cup sliced mushrooms**
- **½ cup sliced water chestnuts**
- **1 cup baby corn**
- **½ cup sliced chives**
- **½ batch pie dough (opposite)**

- In a small bowl combine 1 tablespoon of water, the soy sauce, sesame oil, sherry, chili sauce and oyster sauce, if using. Combine the cornstarch and ¼ cup water and set aside.
- Heat the oil in a wok or frying pan, add the ginger and garlic and stir-fry until fragrant. Add the carrots, chayotes, bok choy, mushrooms and water chestnuts and stir-fry until the vegetables are just tender.
- Add the corn, chives and soy sauce mixture and stir well. Add the cornstarch mixture and cook until thick. Remove from heat and leave to cool.
- Preheat oven to 375°F.
- Divide the dough into 12 equal pieces. Roll each piece into a 4 inch circle and place about 1 tablespoon of filling in the center of the lower half. Fold over and seal, pinching the edges together, using a little water if necessary. Place on a greased baking sheet.
- Repeat until all dough and filling are used up.
- Bake for 15–20 minutes until lightly browned.

Makes 12

Note
Chinese chili sauce is available from Chinese food stores and the Chinese section of supermarkets.

Onion Pakoras

- 1½ cups chickpea flour (besan)
- 2 tsp ground roasted cumin (geera)
- 1 tsp salt
- ¾ tsp hot pepper or cayenne
- ½ tsp baking soda
- ¼ cup chopped cilantro (chadon beni)
- 1 large potato, peeled and grated
- 2 medium onions, thinly sliced
- vegetable oil for frying

- In a mixing bowl combine the chickpea flour with the cumin, salt, pepper and baking soda. Stir in ⅔ cup cold water.
- Add the potato, onion and cilantro. Stir to combine.
- Drop the batter by spoonfuls into hot oil and fry on both sides for about 2–3 minutes.
- Drain well.

Makes about 18

Eggplant Pakoras

- Use 1 small eggplant, cut into cubes, and 2 tablespoons minced ginger in place of the potato and onion.

Vegetable Pakoras

- **1 cup chickpea flour (besan)**
- **½ tsp baking soda**
- **1 tsp chili powder**
- **1 tsp salt**
- **1 tsp freshly ground black pepper**
- **1 tsp ground roasted cumin (geera)**
- **½ tsp saffron powder**
- **2 tbs finely chopped cilantro (chadon beni)**
- **vegetable oil for frying**
- **4 cups fresh vegetables, cut into bite-sized portions**

- Place the first eight ingredients in a bowl, add ½ cup ice cold water and stir to form a thick batter, almost the consistency of pancake batter.
- Heat oil in a wok. Dip the vegetable pieces into the batter, drop into the hot oil and quickly fry. Do not let the vegetables remain too long in the pan as they will become soggy.
- Drain on paper towels and serve immediately with a yogurt dip.

Serves 4–6

Bake or Fry
Crab 'n' Cassava Cakes

- **12 oz cassava (yuca), peeled**
- **12 oz crab meat, picked over**
- **1 cup grated red onion**
- **½ cup finely chopped parsley**
- **½ cup chopped cilantro (chadon beni)**
- **½ cup bread crumbs**
- **1 tsp pepper sauce**
- **1 tsp grated ginger**
- **1 tsp minced garlic**
- **4 tbs fresh lime juice**
- **salt**
- **vegetable oil for frying**

- Grate the cassava very finely. This will release some of the starchy juices, which will help the mixture to bind. Combine the cassava with all the remaining ingredients except the oil and mix well.
- Heat the oil in a non-stick frying pan.
- With your hands, form the cassava mixture into cakes about 2–3 inches in diameter. Gently pan fry until golden and cooked through on each side. Drain.
- Serve with ginger orange dip.

Makes 12–15

For a lighter dish
To bake the crab cakes: preheat oven to 350ºF. Place the crab cakes onto an oiled baking sheet and bake for 5 minutes, until crisp at the bottom. Turn and set oven to broil. Broil until golden, brush with oil and remove.

Ginger Orange Dip

- **½ cup good quality English marmalade**
- **2 tbs Chinese chili sauce**
- **½ tsp grated ginger**
- **2 tbs rice vinegar**

- Combine all the ingredients and stir.

Makes about ½ cup

Hot 'n' Spicy Wings

The spicy sauce in this recipe will keep in the refrigerator for about a week.

FOR THE SAUCE
- 2 tbs vegetable oil
- 4 garlic cloves, minced
- 2 onions, minced
- 1 hot pepper, seeded and chopped (or to taste)
- ½ green bell pepper, chopped
- ¼ cup finely chopped celery
- ½ cup ketchup
- 2 tbs brown sugar
- 3 tbs white vinegar
- 3 tbs Worcestershire sauce
- 1 tbs chili powder

FOR THE WINGS
- 16 chicken wings, split into wing and small drumstick
- 1 tbs minced garlic
- 1 tbs minced chives
- 1 tbs fresh lime juice

• Heat the oil in a saucepan. Add the garlic, onion, peppers and celery and sauté until fragrant. Add the remaining ingredients and simmer for 10–15 minutes until thick and bubbly.

• Remove the wing tip from the wings (keep to use in stock). Marinate the wings and small drumsticks in the garlic, chives and lime juice, with some salt and freshly ground black pepper. Let stand for about 30 minutes.

• Preheat oven to 375ºF.

• Place the wings in an ovenproof baking tray or dish and bake for about 20 minutes, turning once, until lightly browned.

• Remove from the oven, baste with the sauce, then return to the oven for about 5 minutes more. Serve hot.

Serves 4

Shrimp Pâté with Rum & Fresh Herbs

- **2 tbs unsalted butter**
- **6 slices bread, ends trimmed and cut into shapes**

FOR THE PÂTÉ

- **1 lb shrimp, peeled and deveined**
- **¼ cup minced fresh herbs**
- **½ cup unsalted butter, softened**
- **½ cup cream cheese, softened**
- **2 tbs lemon juice or 1 tbs lime juice**
- **1 tsp pepper sauce**
- **1 tbs rum**
- **pinch of grated nutmeg**
- **½ tsp powdered mustard**

- Bring ½ cup water to a boil, add the shrimp and herbs, and cook for 5 minutes or until the shrimp are pink and curled. Drain the water and purée the shrimp and herbs in a food processor.
- Combine the shrimp mixture with the remaining pâté ingredients and add salt and pepper to taste. Spoon into small bowls and refrigerate.
- To make toasts, melt the butter in a saucepan, then brown the bread shapes in the butter to toast evenly.
- Serve the pâté with the toast.

Makes 24; serves 10 as a dip

Beef Pies

- **1 tsp salt**
- **2 cups flour**
- **⅔ cup shortening**
- **¼ cup ice water**
- **1 egg, beaten**

FOR THE FILLING
- **2 tbs vegetable oil**
- **1 cup chopped fresh herbs (chives, thyme, celery, parsley)**
- **2 garlic cloves, chopped**
- **2 pimento peppers, seeded and chopped**
- **½ hot pepper, seeded and chopped**
- **1 onion, chopped**
- **1 lb ground beef**
- **broth, if necessary (see method)**
- **2 slices bread, crumbled**

• To make the pastry: place the salt and flour into a mixing bowl.
Add shortening and rub into the flour until the mixture resembles fine crumbs. Add the ice water a little at a time to bring the dough together. You may not need to add all the water. Refrigerate for 30 minutes.

• To make the filling: heat the oil in a frying pan. Add the herbs, garlic, peppers and onion. Sauté until tender, about 4 minutes, then add the beef and cook until no longer pink, about 5 minutes. Add a little broth or water to moisten if necessary.

• If the beef seems lumpy put it into a food processor bowl and process for 30 seconds, just until fine.

• Add the crumbled bread and combine. Season with salt and freshly ground black pepper to taste.
Leave to cool.

• Preheat oven to 375°F.

• Divide the dough into two. Roll each piece to about ¼ inch thickness.
Cut out rounds with a 3 inch cutter.

• Place about 1 teaspoon of filling onto half the rounds. Cover with the remaining rounds and seal. Brush with beaten egg and bake for 15 minutes until golden.

Makes 24

Conch Fritters

- 1 lb conch, skin removed, tenderized and chopped (see page 63)
- 2 eggs
- 4 garlic cloves
- 1 pimento pepper, seeded and chopped
- ½ cup chopped fresh herbs (parsley, thyme, chives)
- 1 cup flour
- 2 tsp baking powder
- 1 tsp salt
- ¼ cup milk, if necessary (see method)
- vegetable oil for frying

• Place the conch into a food processor and mince. Add the eggs, garlic, pimento and herbs and process to incorporate all the ingredients.
• Remove mixture to a bowl and add the flour, baking powder and salt. Stir well to combine: your mixture should be like a paste, but not too runny. If the mixture seems too dry, add a little milk.
• Heat the oil in a frying pan and drop the mixture by teaspoonfuls into the hot oil. Fry until puffed and golden, about 5–6 minutes.
• Drain and serve with chili mayo dip.

Makes about 24

Chili Mayo Dip

- ¾ cup low fat mayonnaise
- 1 tbs horseradish sauce
- 1 tsp chili powder
- 1 tsp pepper sauce
- ¼ cup chopped parsley
- 1 tbs fresh lime juice

• Combine all the ingredients and stir well. Serve with fritters.

Makes about 1 cup

Cassava &
Salt Cod Brandade

The traditional Mediterranean classic is made with
salt cod and potatoes. Here, I've used cassava for an earthy
and delicious brandade.
Serve with triangles of toast for a delicious appetizer.

- **4 oz salt cod**
- **½ lime**
- **⅓ cup olive oil**
- **⅓ cup milk, plus ½ cup**
- **2 garlic cloves**
- **1 hot pepper**
- **2 tbs butter**
- **1 lb cassava (yuca),
  boiled and inner vein removed**
- **¼ cup chopped chives**

• Squeeze lime juice onto the salt
cod and boil in enough fresh water
to cover until tender, about 5–10
minutes. Remove from pan and flake.
• Heat the olive oil and ⅓ cup milk
separately.
• Place the fish in a blender or
food processor and purée. Add the
garlic and pepper. With the motor
running, add the warmed milk and oil
alternately, and process to a creamy
consistency. Remove and set aside.
• Preheat oven to 350°F.
• Heat the butter with ½ cup milk and
add to the cassava.
• Mash to a creamy consistency – a
hand-held mixer works well here. Add
the chives and combine. Add salt and
freshly ground black pepper to taste.
• Combine the cassava with the salt
fish mixture and mix well.
• Put into a shallow pie plate and
bake for about 15 minutes until
browned on top.

Serves 6–8

Batter-fried Cauliflower with Curry & Cumin

Serve these crisp cauliflower pieces with a spicy yogurt dip.

- **vegetable oil for frying**
- **1 cauliflower,
  cut into segments**

FOR THE BATTER
- **1 cup flour**
- **1 tsp baking powder**
- **1 egg**
- **½ cup water**
- **1 tsp cumin (geera)**
- **1 tsp curry powder**
- **1 tsp salt**
- **⅓ cup chopped cilantro
  (chadon beni)**
- **1 tsp freshly ground black pepper**

- Combine all the ingredients for the batter and stir well to a smooth consistency.
- Heat the oil in a deep pot.
- Dip the cauliflower pieces into the batter and fry in the hot oil until golden and tender.
- Drain and serve.

Serves 4–6

Roasted Eggplant Dip

The Syrian Lebanese population in the Caribbean has brought in
an Eastern Mediterranean influence to our shores, as in this dip,
which can be served with pita bread.

- **1 large eggplant**
- **1 garlic clove**
- **1 tsp sesame oil**
- **1 tbs fresh lime juice**
- **1 tbs plain yogurt**
- **½ tsp ground roasted
  cumin (geera)**

GARNISH
- **chopped parsley**
- **olive oil**

- Roast the eggplant over an open flame until tender, about 8–10 minutes.
- Remove the pulp and place in a food processor. Add the garlic, sesame oil, lime juice, yogurt, cumin, and salt and freshly ground black pepper. Process until blended.
- Place on a platter, sprinkle with chopped parsley and drizzle with oil.

Serves 4–6

Carnival Fish Pies

- **vegetable oil for frying**

FOR THE DOUGH
- **2 cups all-purpose flour**
- **2 tsp baking powder**
- **½ tsp salt**
- **4 tbs shortening**

FOR THE FILLING
- **1 lb fish fillets, steamed**
- **1 tsp hot pepper sauce**
- **1 tsp fresh lime juice**
- **½ cup finely chopped fresh herbs (parsley, thyme, cilantro, chives)**
- **1 large potato, peeled, boiled and crushed**
- **2 large garlic cloves, minced**
- **salt and freshly ground black pepper**

- To make the dough: combine the flour, baking powder, salt and shortening. Add water to make a soft but pliable and non-sticky dough. Knead into a ball and leave to rest for 15 minutes.
- Divide the dough into 10 pieces, and roll each piece into a ball. Rest for 5 minutes.
- To make the filling: flake the fish and remove any bones. Add all the other ingredients and mix well. Taste and adjust seasoning.
- Roll each piece of dough into a 5 inch circle. Place about 1–2 tablespoons of the filling onto the lower portion of each circle, and bring the upper portion over the lower portion to cover in a half moon shape. Seal.
- Heat the oil in a frying pan and shallow fry the pies until golden brown.
- Drain and serve with chadon beni pesto (page 311)

Makes 10

Fish Fritters

- **4 cups steamed fish**
- **⅓ cup chopped cilantro (chadon beni) (optional)**
- **⅓ cup chopped chives**
- **2 pimento peppers, seeded and chopped**
- **3 tbs fresh lime juice**
- **1½ tsp salt**
- **1 tsp freshly ground black pepper**
- **2 cups flour**
- **2 tsp baking powder**
- **1½–2 cups milk**
- **vegetable oil for frying**

- Place the fish in a large mixing bowl. Pick out any bones and add the herbs, peppers, lime juice, salt and pepper.
- Add the flour and baking powder. Stir in the milk gradually to make a stiff but soft batter, being careful not to crush the fish.
- Heat the oil in a deep frying pan and drop the batter by teaspoonfuls into the hot oil. Fry until golden and puffed.
- Serve hot.

Makes about 24–30

Caribbean Shrimp Cocktail

- **24 medium shrimp, peeled and deveined**
- **1 tsp ground Spanish thyme**
- **½ tsp salt**
- **2 cups shredded lettuce**
- **lime slices to garnish**

FOR THE SAUCE
- **½ cup tomato ketchup**
- **¼ cup fresh lime juice**
- **1 tsp Worcestershire sauce**
- **1 tsp pepper sauce**
- **⅛ tsp allspice powder**
- **¼ tsp sugar**
- **1 tsp minced onion**
- **1 tbs minced cilantro (chadon beni)**
- **salt to taste**

● Marinate the shrimp in the Spanish thyme and salt for 15 minutes.
● Steam the shrimp in about ½ cup water. When they are pink and curled, drain and refrigerate.
● Combine all the ingredients for the sauce.
● Place the lettuce into four stemmed glasses.
● Combine the shrimp with the sauce and divide equally between the glasses. Garnish with lime slices.
● Serve immediately or refrigerate until required.

Serves 4

Seafood Cheescake with Fresh Herbs

This cheesecake may be baked without the crust and served with crackers.

- **2 x 8 oz packages cream cheese**
- **3 eggs**
- **¾ cup all-purpose flour**
- **½ lb cooked crab meat, picked over**
- **⅓ cup chopped chives**
- **¼ cup chopped fresh herbs (thyme, parsley, basil)**
- **2 garlic cloves, minced**
- **1 tsp hot pepper sauce**
- **1 cup sour cream or yogurt**

FOR THE CRUST
- **¾ cup crackers, crushed**
- **2 tbs melted butter**

- Preheat oven to 325°F.
- To make the crust: process the cracker crumbs to a fine consistency and add the butter. Press into the bottom of an 8 inch springform cheesecake pan.
- Bake for 5 minutes, remove and refrigerate.
- Cream the cheese in a mixer bowl until smooth. Add the eggs one at a time and beat until smooth. Add the flour and combine, then fold in the crab, herbs, garlic, pepper sauce and salt and freshly ground black pepper to taste. Fold in the sour cream and mix.
- Pour into the prepared crust and bake for about 45–55 minutes until firm and lightly browned.
- Refrigerate until chilled.

Serves 10

Stuffed Crab Backs with Parsley Parmesan Gratin

- **1 tbs fresh lime juice**
- **1 lb fresh crab meat, picked over**
- **2 tbs butter**
- **2 onions, minced**
- **2 garlic cloves, minced**
- **½ cup finely chopped chives, white and green parts**
- **2 tbs fresh French thyme**
- **1 tbs chopped celery**
- **2 pimento peppers, seeded and chopped**
- **1 hot pepper, seeded and chopped**
- **1½ cups soft bread crumbs**
- **6 crab shells**

FOR THE GRATIN
- **1 cup toasted bread crumbs**
- **2 tbs chopped celery**
- **2 tbs Parmesan cheese**
- **2 tbs softened butter**

- Preheat oven to 375°F.
- Add the lime juice to the crab meat and combine.
- Melt the butter in a sauté pan, add the onion and garlic and cook until translucent, about 4 minutes. Add the chives, thyme, celery, pimentos and hot pepper and cook for a further 4 minutes.
- Turn off the heat, add the crab meat and turn into a large bowl. Mix to combine, add the bread crumbs and stir. Season with salt.
- To make the gratin: combine all the ingredients until the crumbs become coated with the butter.
- Spoon the crab meat into the crab shells and top with the gratin.
- Bake for about 15 minutes, until the gratin is lightly browned.

Serves 6

soups & salads

Traditional Caribbean soups are hearty, thick and very satisfying – usually a Saturday lunch ritual. I've lightened the soups up in this section by offering spicy and hearty soups without the addition of provisions, like smoky split pea soup, Tobago pigeon pea soup, spicy shrimp bisque and conch chowder.

There are two traditional favorites: cowheel soup and oxtail soup with dumplings. Caribbean gazpacho with avocado is a refreshing alternative on a hot day, as is the cream of cucumber soup. The salads in this section use local herbs, seafood, fruits and vegetables together with a suggestion of the Mediterranean, as in roasted beet and onion salad with balsamic vinaigrette, and chickpea and tomato salad. The tropical overtones in the green papaya salad, seafood salad, tomato avocado salad and sweet and sour Caribbean slaw are sure to bring a burst of color and flavor to your meal!

Spicy Shrimp Bisque

- 2 tbs butter
- 1 onion, finely chopped
- 4 garlic cloves, minced
- 1 tbs chopped celery
- ½ hot pepper, seeded and chopped
- 1 pimento pepper, seeded and chopped
- 1 lb small shrimp, peeled and deveined
- 4 cups broth
- 1 tbs minced chives
- 1 tsp French thyme
- ¼ cup chopped parsley
- 2 leaves Spanish thyme
- 2 tbs sherry or rum

FOR THE ROUX
- 2 tbs unsalted butter
- 1 tbs flour

- Melt the butter in a large soup pot. Add the onion, garlic, celery and peppers and cook until fragrant. Add the shrimp and cook until pink and curled.
- Add the broth and cook for about 35 minutes.
- Meanwhile, make the roux: melt the butter in a saucepan, add the flour and cook until light brown in color. Set aside.
- Add the herbs to the soup mixture, then pour soup into a food processor and chop very fine.
- Return to the pot, bring to a boil and thicken by stirring in a small amount of roux at a time.
- Stir in the sherry. Taste and adjust seasoning.

Serves 4

Smoked Green Split Pea Soup

Smoked bones add a great flavor to this soup – you can use smoked chicken bones instead of beef if you prefer.

- **1 cup green split peas**
- **1 garlic clove, minced**
- **1 large pimento pepper, seeded and chopped**
- **smoked beef bones (optional)**
- **¼ tsp ground cloves**
- **1 cup chopped chives**
- **1 tbs French thyme**
- **1 hot pepper (optional)**
- **6 cups chicken or vegetable stock**
- **salt and freshly ground black pepper to taste**
- **1 tbs butter**

• Combine all the ingredients except the butter in a large soup pot, bring to a boil and then cover and simmer until the peas are cooked, about 40 minutes.
• Remove the beef bones, if using. Purée soup if desired, then return to heat and stir in butter.

Serves 4–6

SOUPS AND SALADS

Cream of Cauliflower Soup

- **4 tbs butter**
- **1 cup minced onions**
- **1 tsp minced garlic**
- **¼ cup flour**
- **1 large head of cauliflower, washed and cut into pieces**
- **8 cups broth**
- **1 cup evaporated milk**
- **½ cup grated Parmesan cheese**

• Melt the butter in a soup pot. Add the onions and garlic and sauté for 5 minutes until tender.
• Stir in the flour and cook until smooth, without browning, about 2 minutes.
• Add the cauliflower and cook for a few minutes, then add the broth and season with salt and freshly ground black pepper. Bring to a boil, cover and simmer for 30 minutes.
• Purée the soup and return to the pot. Add the milk, then reheat and stir in the cheese.

Serves 4–6

For a lighter dish
Use regular or low fat evaporated milk.

Yellow Split Pea Soup with Chili

- **8 cups broth**
- **1 cup yellow split peas, washed and picked over**
- **3–4 smoked chicken bones**
- **4 garlic cloves**
- **1 cup chopped pumpkin**
- **1 cup chopped carrots**
- **½ cup chopped chives**
- **¼ cup celery**
- **¼ cup thyme**
- **2 tbs butter**
- **1 tbs chili powder**

● Put the broth, peas and bones into a soup pot, add the garlic and boil for about 30 minutes.
● Remove the bones and add the pumpkin, carrots, chives, celery and thyme. Bring to a boil and simmer for 15 more minutes until tender. Season to taste with salt and freshly ground black pepper.
● Purée the soup, return to the pot and add the butter and chili powder. Stir to mix.
● Reheat before serving.

Serves 4–6

Oxtail Soup with Cinnamon Dumplings

- 1 tbs ground herb seasoning
- 2 lb lean oxtail, jointed
- 1 tbs vegetable oil
- 3 garlic cloves, minced
- 1 large onion, chopped
- ⅓ cup chopped chives
- 2 tbs chopped celery
- 1 pimento pepper, seeded and chopped
- 2 sprigs of thyme
- ½ lb pumpkin, peeled and cubed
- 1 hot pepper
- 2 lb provisions (sweet potato, taro root), cut into 2 inch pieces
- cinnamon dumplings (see right)

• Rub the herb seasoning onto the oxtail and marinate for about 30 minutes.

• Add the oil to a large soup pot and sear oxtail on both sides to brown. Add the garlic, onion, chives, celery, pimento pepper and thyme. Cover with about 8 cups water and boil until oxtail is tender, 1 hour.

• Skim off any fat and froth from the surface. Add more water if you need to and bring the soup back to a boil. Add the pumpkin and hot pepper and cook for another 15 minutes until tender. Add provisions, stir, and cook for 15 more minutes.

• Meanwhile, divide the dumpling dough into 4 pieces. Roll each piece into a log 1 inch thick and cut into 1 inch pieces.

• Add to the boiling soup and cook for about 5 minutes, or until the dumplings rise to the top. Season with salt and freshly ground black pepper. Remove the hot pepper before serving.

Serves 4–6

Cinnamon Dumplings

- 2 cups flour
- 1 tsp baking powder
- 1 tsp cinnamon
- ½ tsp salt
- 2 tsp butter

• Combine the flour, baking powder, cinnamon and salt in a large bowl. Rub in the butter and add enough water to make a firm dough. Knead for a few minutes. Cover and let rest for about 30 minutes.

• Use as required in recipe.

Cream of Cucumber Soup

- **3 tbs butter**
- **1 onion, chopped**
- **3 cucumbers, peeled and sliced**
- **3 tbs flour**
- **3 cups vegetable or chicken stock**
- **1 cup milk**
- **chopped mint or chives to garnish**

- Melt 2 tablespoons of the butter in a medium-sized saucepan and sauté the onion and cucumbers until the cucumbers become tender and the onions are fragrant. Remove from pan.
- Melt the rest of the butter and add the flour. Cook to a smooth roux, add stock and stir over a low heat until thick. Season with salt and freshly ground black pepper to taste.
- Return the cucumbers and onion to the pan and cook for a further 10 minutes.
- Purée soup in a blender. Just before serving, reheat and stir in the milk.
- Garnish with chopped mint or chives.

Serves 4–6

Cowheel Soup with Provisions

Saturday soup is popular on the islands.
This version is a tradition, especially in Trinidad – healthy,
nourishing and very satisfying!

- 2 lb cowheels, cleaned
- 1 tbs minced chives plus
  ⅓ cup chopped chives
- 1 tbs fresh thyme plus 2 sprigs
- ½ tbs minced celery
- 3 garlic cloves, minced
- 1 large onion, chopped
- 1 pimento pepper,
  seeded and chopped
- 1 hot pepper
- 2 lb provisions (see page 157),
  peeled and cut into 2 inch pieces
- 1 tsp freshly ground black pepper

- Rub the cowheels with the minced chives, thyme and celery. Place into a large soup pot and cover with about 8 cups water. Add the garlic, onion, chopped chives, peppers and thyme sprigs. Boil until cowheels are tender, about 2 hours.
- Remove any excess fat, add provisions and cook until tender, about 15 minutes. Season with the black pepper and salt to taste. Remove the hot pepper before serving.

Serves 4–6

Note
Cowheels are available from West Indian food stores. When cooked, they are very gluey in texture and full of protein.

Tobago Pigeon Pea Soup

This recipe was inspired by a pigeon pea soup I enjoyed while staying at Kariwak Village in Tobago.

- **2 tbs vegetable oil**
- **2 garlic cloves, chopped**
- **2 onions, chopped**
- **¼ cup chopped celery**
- **¼ cup chopped chives**
- **1 large sprig of fresh thyme**
- **4 oz pumpkin, chopped**
- **1 carrot, chopped**
- **1 lb fresh pigeon peas or 14 oz can**
- **½ cup freshly made tomato sauce**
- **2 cloves**
- **1 hot pepper**
- **4 cups chicken or vegetable stock**
- **½ tsp sugar**

- Heat the oil in a large soup pot and add the garlic and onion. Sauté until fragrant and tender, about 4 minutes.
- Add the celery, chives and thyme, and stir to combine. Add the pumpkin and carrot, stir, and add the pigeon peas. Stir well. Add the tomato sauce, cloves and hot pepper and cook for a few minutes more.
- Stir in the stock, sugar, and salt and freshly ground black pepper to taste. Bring to a boil, cover and simmer for about 20–30 minutes if using canned peas, 45 minutes if using fresh peas.
- Remove the hot pepper. Purée half the soup in a blender.
- Return to the pot and stir, adding a little more stock or water to thin if necessary. Bring to a boil once again before serving.

Serves 4–6 as a main course

Gingery Pumpkin Soup

Adding ginger to this soup gives it a very exotic flavor.

- **2 lb calabaza pumpkin**
- **2 tbs vegetable oil or butter**
- **1 onion, diced**
- **4 garlic cloves, chopped**
- **2 inch piece of ginger, peeled and chopped**
- **5 cups chicken or vegetable stock**
- **⅓ cup chopped chives**
- **¼ tsp allspice powder**
- **½ cup evaporated milk (optional)**

- Peel the pumpkin and cut into 1 inch chunks.
- Heat the oil in a large saucepan or Dutch oven over medium heat. Add the onion and garlic, and sauté for about 4 minutes until fragrant and tender.
- Add the ginger and cook until fragrant. Add the pumpkin, stock, chives and allspice, and bring to a boil.
- Cover and simmer until the pumpkin is tender, about 30–40 minutes.
- Purée the soup in a blender or food processor.
- Return soup to saucepan, add milk, if using, and heat through. Season with salt and freshly ground black pepper.

Serves 6

Conch Chowder

Conch, or lambie as it is also called, is a popular seafood in the Caribbean, from the French Caribbean, through the Bahamas, Grenades and as far south as Trinidad and Tobago.
It is eaten in many ways: stewed or fricasseed, curried, in fritters, soused and in this flavorful chowder.

- **1 tbs vegetable oil**
- **1 small onion**
- **1 tbs chopped celery**
- **½ hot pepper, chopped**
- **½ bell pepper, seeded and chopped**
- **2 garlic cloves**
- **1 potato, peeled and cubed**
- **1 small carrot, chopped**
- **½ cup coconut milk**
- **½ cup milk**
- **½ tsp saffron powder**
- **pinch of grated nutmeg**
- **pinch of allspice powder**
- **1 lb conch, skin removed, tenderized and chopped (see below)**

● Heat the oil in a saucepan, add the onion, celery, peppers and garlic. Stir to combine. Cook for about 3–4 minutes, add potato and carrot, stir to combine.

● Combine 3 cups water with the coconut milk, milk, saffron powder, nutmeg and allspice. Add to the saucepan and bring to a boil.

● Add the conch and cook until almost boiling. Season with salt and freshly ground black pepper, cover and simmer for 30 minutes until potato is tender.

Serves 4

TO PREPARE CONCH

● Place conch in a large bowl filled with cool water. Squeeze the juice of 1 lime into the bowl.

● Remove the conch, and tear or cut away the blackish and orange skin.

● Cut into smaller pieces and pound with a meat pounder until the meat is broken.

● Wash in limed water again, then cut into small cubes and prepare as the recipe suggests.

Caribbean Gazpacho with Avocado & Lime

- **28 oz can whole tomatoes**
- **1 tbs fresh lime juice**
- **½ hot pepper, seeded and chopped**
- **1 garlic clove**
- **1 tsp salt**
- **½ tsp dried oregano**
- **1 cup tomato juice**
- **1 tbs olive oil**
- **½ tsp sugar**
- **¼ cup chopped celery**
- **1 small cucumber, chopped**
- **¼ cup chopped onion, soaked in cold water for ½ hour**
- **¼ cup chopped green bell pepper**
- **¼ cup sliced olives**
- **¼ cup chopped cilantro (chadon beni)**
- **1 small avocado, peeled and diced**

- In a blender, purée the tomatoes with their juice, the lime juice, hot pepper, garlic, salt, oregano and tomato juice.
- Stir in the oil, sugar, celery, cucumber, onion and bell pepper. Sprinkle with the olives and cilantro.
- Chill before serving. Stir in the avocado just before serving.

Serves 6–8

Sweet & Sour Caribbean Slaw

- **2 cups grated red cabbage**
- **1 cup grated green cabbage**
- **1 carrot, grated**
- **1 red onion, grated**
- **1 bell pepper, julienned**
- **1 tbs sesame seeds**

FOR THE DRESSING
- **1 cup white vinegar**
- **⅓ cup brown sugar**
- **2 garlic cloves, minced**
- **1 tsp sesame oil**

- Put all the vegetables into a salad bowl.
- To make the dressing: bring the vinegar to a boil, add the sugar and cook for 1 minute until the sugar dissolves. Stir in the garlic and sesame oil.
- Cool, then pour onto salad and toss.
- Sprinkle with sesame seeds.

Serves 6

Green Papaya Salad

- **1 green papaya, about 4 lb**
- **1 carrot, grated**
- **1 tomato, seeded and cut into strips**
- **1 hot pepper, seeded and julienned**
- **⅓ cup cilantro (chadon beni)**
- **⅓ cup mint**
- **⅓ cup basil**
- **⅓ cup chopped peanuts (optional)**

FOR THE DRESSING
- **1 garlic clove, minced**
- **3 tbs fresh lime juice**
- **1 tbs soy sauce**
- **½ tsp sesame oil**
- **1 tbs brown sugar**

- Peel and coarsely grate the papaya and place in a colander to drain off any excess juices.
- Put in a salad bowl and combine with the carrot, tomato, hot pepper and fresh herbs. Add salt to taste.
- To make the dressing: combine all the ingredients and stir. Pour over the salad and toss gently. Sprinkle with peanuts if using.
- Refrigerate until ready for use.

Serves 4–6

Tomato Avocado Salad

- **4 large ripe tomatoes, peeled, seeded and chopped**
- **½ green bell pepper**
- **1 small onion**
- **2 tbs olive oil**
- **2 tbs fresh lime juice**
- **1 garlic clove, minced**
- **½ tsp sugar**
- **⅓ cup chopped chives**
- **1 avocado, cut into ½ inch pieces**
- **1 tbs cilantro (chadon beni)**

- Finely chop the tomatoes and set aside.
- Finely chop the bell pepper and onion in a food processor and add to the tomatoes.
- Combine the olive oil, lime juice, garlic, sugar and some salt. Whisk well or emulsify with a food processor or blender.
- Pour onto the tomato mixture, add chives and stir.
- Refrigerate for about 1 hour until ready for use.
- Add the avocado, toss gently, and sprinkle on the cilantro.

Serves 4

Sweet Potato Salad

Sweet potatoes are delightful when dressed with lemon herb vinaigrette.

- **1 lb sweet potatoes**
- **1 cup chopped fresh herbs (basil, chives, cilantro, parsley)**
- **1 large red or green bell pepper, seeded and cut into strips**

FOR THE VINAIGRETTE
- **juice of 1 lemon or 3 tbs fresh lemon juice**
- **¼ cup sunflower oil**
- **1 tsp Dijon mustard**
- **1 garlic clove, minced**
- **salt and freshly ground black pepper**

- Combine all the ingredients for the vinaigrette and set aside.
- Boil or roast the sweet potatoes until tender, drain, and cool. Peel and cut into 1 inch cubes.
- Combine the herbs, pepper and potatoes. Toss with the vinaigrette and adjust seasoning to taste.
- Chill before serving.

Serves 4–6

Tropical Fruit Salad with Brown Sugar Passion Fruit Syrup

Tropical fruits are delightful when dressed with this delicious brown sugar syrup.

- **1 small watermelon, flesh cut into chunks**
- **18 cups assorted fresh fruit (mango, papaya, carambola, pineapple, grapes, bananas), cut into chunks**

FOR THE SYRUP
- **1 vanilla bean**
- **1 cup brown sugar**
- **⅓ cup passion fruit pulp**

- To make the syrup: slit the vanilla bean in two, scrape seeds from the pod and place in a saucepan with the sugar and ⅓ cup water. Boil until bubbly then continue cooking until the sugar is dissolved and the mixture is thick.
- Remove from heat, cool and add passion fruit pulp.
- Place the fruit into a large glass serving bowl, spoon syrup onto fruit and gently toss.
- Refrigerate until ready to serve.

Serves 20

Breadfruit Salad with Cilantro, Parsley & Chives

- **3–4 lb breadfruit, boiled, cooled and cut into ½ inch cubes**
- **1 red bell pepper, seeded and finely chopped**
- **1 cup low fat mayonnaise**
- **⅓ cup chopped cilantro (chadon beni)**
- **⅓ cup chopped parsley**
- **¼ cup chopped chives**
- **juice of 1 large lemon**
- **salt and freshly ground black pepper**

- Place breadfruit in a bowl. Add the chopped bell pepper.
- Combine the mayonnaise with all the other ingredients and stir.
- Add to the breadfruit and stir to combine. Cover and refrigerate until ready for use.

Serves 6–8

Provision Salad

- **4 lb provisions (taro root, yams, sweet potatoes), peeled, boiled and cut into cubes**
- **¼ cup diced sweet red bell pepper**
- **¼ cup diced celery stalks**
- **¼ cup chopped fresh chives**
- **¼ cup minced parsley**
- **½ tsp fresh oregano**
- **½ tsp paprika**
- **⅔ cup olive or vegetable oil**
- **⅓ cup red wine vinegar**
- **1 tsp minced garlic**
- **1 tbs Dijon mustard**

- Combine the provisions with the diced pepper, celery, chives, parsley, oregano and paprika.
- In a small bowl, combine the oil with the vinegar, garlic, mustard, and salt and freshly ground black pepper to taste. Blend to make a thick emulsion.
- Combine with the provision mixture and toss to coat evenly.
- Garnish with parsley and refrigerate until ready for use.

Serves 10

Chickpea & Tomato Salad

Chickpeas are popular on the islands – we love to eat them curried, or crispy fried as a snack. In this salad they are not only healthy but delicious as well!

- **2 x 14 oz cans chickpeas, drained and rinsed**
- **4 salad tomatoes, seeded and chopped**
- **½ cup chopped fresh herbs (chives, cilantro, basil, mint)**

FOR THE DRESSING
- **4 garlic cloves**
- **½ tsp paprika**
- **4 tbs red wine vinegar**
- **4 tbs fresh lime juice**
- **½ cup vegetable oil**
- **2 rounded teaspoons ground roasted cumin (geera)**
- **salt and freshly ground black pepper**

- Place the first three ingredients in a bowl.
- Combine all the ingredients for the dressing in a blender and process until well blended.
- Add to the chickpeas and toss to coat.

Serves 6–8

Roasted Beet
& Pineapple Salad

- **2 cups pineapple chunks**
- **4 large beets, roasted or boiled (see below)**
- **2 pimento peppers, seeded and finely chopped**
- **½ cup chopped chives**
- **½ cup chopped parsley**

FOR THE DRESSING
- **2 garlic cloves**
- **2 tbs fresh lime juice**
- **⅓ cup olive oil**
- **salt and freshly ground black pepper**

TO ROAST BEETS
- **Wash beets and wrap in aluminum foil. Roast in a preheated 350ºF oven for about 60 minutes until tender, depending on the size of the beets. Cool and peel.**

- Combine all the ingredients for the dressing. Stir or shake well and set aside.
- Finely chop the pineapple and place in a large glass bowl. Peel the beets and dice finely. Add to pineapple together with the peppers.
- Pour on the dressing, toss, add chives and refrigerate until ready for use.
- Before serving, add parsley and toss again.

Serves 6

Roasted Beet & Onion Salad with Balsamic Vinaigrette

- **4 medium onions**
- **4 medium beets, washed**
- **1 large sprig of fresh French thyme**
- **½ tsp freshly ground black pepper**
- **2 tsp balsamic vinegar**
- **2 tbs olive oil**

FOR THE BALSAMIC VINAIGRETTE
- **3 tbs balsamic vinegar**
- **1 garlic clove, minced**
- **⅓ cup olive oil**

- Preheat oven to 350ºF.
- Peel onions and lightly score at top.
- Place beets and onions onto some heavy-duty aluminum foil.
- Combine pepper, balsamic vinegar and olive oil. Drizzle onto the beets and onions. Top with the sprig of thyme and wrap securely.
- Bake until tender, about 60 minutes. Remove from oven and cool.
- Peel beets and slice. Arrange on a platter topped with onions.
- To make the vinaigrette: combine the vinegar with the garlic. Whisk in the olive oil and season with salt and freshly ground black pepper.
- Drizzle the vinaigrette onto the beets and serve warm.

Serves 4–6

Salad of Beets, Greens & Feta Cheese

- **8 cups mixed salad greens, cleaned, washed, dried and broken into bite-sized pieces**
- **4 oz feta cheese, crumbled**
- **2 tbs chopped fresh herbs (parsley, basil, chives, cilantro)**
- **1 large ripe tomato, cut into segments**
- **1 cucumber, sliced**
- **1 red onion, thinly sliced**
- **2 beets, roasted and peeled (see page 78)**

FOR THE DRESSING
- **3 tbs red wine vinegar**
- **2 garlic cloves, minced**
- **1 tbs Dijon mustard**
- **½ cup extra virgin olive oil**

• Place the salad greens in a large salad bowl. Sprinkle with the cheese and herbs. Add tomato, cucumber and onion, and toss.

• Add the prepared beets right at the end to avoid discoloration.

• To make the dressing: combine the red wine vinegar, garlic and mustard. Add salt and freshly ground black pepper and gradually whisk in the olive oil until a thick emulsion is formed. Pour over the salad and toss.

Serves 6–8

Mixed Bean Salad

- 14 oz can chickpeas
- 14 oz can red beans
- 10 oz can corn kernels
- 1 red onion, finely chopped
- 4 garlic cloves, chopped
- 1 bell pepper, seeded and chopped
- 1 hot pepper, seeded and chopped
- salt and freshly ground black pepper
- 2 tbs fresh oregano
- ½ cup chopped parsley
- ⅓ cup chopped cilantro
  (chadon beni)

FOR THE DRESSING
- ¼ cup red wine vinegar
- 1 tsp Dijon or other mustard
- 2 garlic cloves, minced
- ¾ cup olive oil
- 1 tbs chopped fresh herbs
- 1 tsp cumin (geera)
- 1 tsp pepper sauce
- ½ tsp salt

● Combine all the ingredients for the dressing and set aside.
● Place all the salad ingredients except the fresh herbs into a glass bowl. Pour on the dressing and toss to combine.
● Refrigerate until ready for use, then add herbs and toss.

Serves 4–6

Party Potato Salad

Potato salad is a favorite dish in the Caribbean but often times it's too soft, with no flavor. My version uses only potatoes with herbs and bell peppers. The dressing is part yogurt, part low fat mayonnaise, making it lighter as well!

- 1 tbs olive oil
- 2 tbs red wine vinegar
- 8 cups diced peeled cooked potatoes (about 10 potatoes)
- 1 cup low fat mayonnaise
- ⅓ cup yogurt
- 1 tbs Dijon mustard
- 1½ tsp salt
- 1 tsp freshly ground black pepper
- ¼ cup chopped celery
- 2 bell peppers, seeded and chopped
- 2 pimento peppers, seeded and chopped
- 1 cup chopped chives
- 2 cups steamed green peas or green beans

- Combine the olive oil with 1 tablespoon of the vinegar and toss with the potatoes.
- Combine the mayonnaise with the remaining vinegar, yogurt, mustard, salt and pepper. Add the chopped celery, peppers, chives and peas. Fold in the potatoes. Mix well and taste and adjust seasonings.
- Cover and refrigerate until ready to serve.

Serves 10–12

Pasta Salad with Feta & Herbs

- **2 cups dried pasta, boiled and drained**
- **1 large bell pepper, seeded and chopped**
- **⅓ cup chopped chives**
- **⅓ cup chopped celery**
- **2 large tomatoes, chopped**
- **2 cucumbers, thinly sliced**
- **4 lettuce leaves, torn into pieces**

FOR THE DRESSING
- **¼ cup crumbled feta cheese**
- **3 tbs red wine vinegar**
- **⅓ cup olive oil**
- **4 garlic cloves, minced**

- In a large salad bowl combine the pasta with the bell pepper, herbs, tomatoes, cucumbers and lettuce.
- Combine all the dressing ingredients and pour onto pasta. Toss to combine. Season with salt and freshly ground black pepper.
- Chill before serving.

Serves 4–6

Seafood Salad

This salad is refreshing and is a perfect appetizer.

- **2 lb assorted seafood, steamed and chilled**
- **1 tbs fresh lime juice**
- **⅓ cup chopped parsley**
- **⅓ cup chopped cilantro (chadon beni)**
- **⅓ cup chopped basil**
- **1 cucumber, thinly sliced**

FOR THE DRESSING
- **⅓ cup olive oil**
- **2 tbs fresh lime juice**
- **2 tbs red wine vinegar**
- **¼ cup tomato ketchup**
- **½ cup mayonnaise**
- **1 tsp freshly ground black pepper**
- **1 tsp Worcestershire sauce**
- **1 tsp sugar**
- **1 tsp Dijon or other mustard**
- **salt**

- Mix the chilled seafood with the lime juice, then combine with the herbs and cucumber.
- Combine all the ingredients for the dressing. Pour onto seafood and toss.
- Chill if not using immediately.

Serves 6

seafood

The warm waters of the Caribbean Sea and Atlantic Ocean give us a wonderful array of fresh seafood to choose from on a daily basis, one of the best things about living in the Caribbean! Fresh fish is sold at the fish markets from the crack of dawn, and a visit there will reveal herring, red snapper, white snapper, white rock salmon, grouper, king fish, ancho, carite and shark – to name just a few. Shrimp from jumbo to salad sized, spiny Caribbean lobster, conch (lambie) and crab are also for sale. Dried and salted fish is also used quite extensively and when we take these back to our kitchens the possibilities for the mode of preparation are endless. Cooking fish the same day it is caught is not unusual here, and the best thing about that is there need not be an extravagant method of preparation. A baked fillet of fresh fish, lightly seasoned with fresh herbs, makes a delicious entrée.

This section reveals some exciting ways to use our local seafood. Fish steaks steamed in banana leaves served with a coconut lemon-grass sauce, lobster grilled and served with a French hot sauce, curried conch, grilled shrimp with a rum and chili glaze, stuffed flying fish fillets; these are just a few of the tantalizing recipes that follow.

87

Grilled Lobster with Sauce Chien

This is a French Caribbean speciality. The lobster is broiled with just a little butter, then enveloped in an aromatic and hot sauce.

- **2 lobsters, live or frozen**
- **2 tbs salt**
- **⅓ cup butter, melted**

- Heat 3 quarts of water in a large pot, add the salt and bring to a boil. Plunge lobsters into water, head first. Cover and heat to boiling, then reduce heat and cook for a further 10–15 minutes. Remove lobsters and drain.
- Preheat broiler or grill.
- Place lobsters on their backs, cut into halves lengthways with a sharp knife. Remove stomach, which is just behind the head, and remove the intestinal vein which runs from the tip of the tail to the stomach. Crack the claws.
- Place the tails meat side up on a baking tray and drizzle with some of the melted butter.
- Grill 3 inches from heat until hot, 2–3 minutes.
- Remove and serve with sauce chien.

Serves 2–3

Sauce Chien

- **1 red onion, peeled and chopped**
- **¼ cup chopped chives**
- **2 garlic cloves, minced**
- **½ hot pepper, seeded and chopped**
- **¼ cup chopped parsley**
- **juice of 2 large limes**
- **2 tbs sunflower oil**
- **1 cup boiling water**

- Combine the first five ingredients. Stir in the lime juice and oil and season with salt and freshly ground black pepper. Pour on the boiling water then cover and leave for 5–10 minutes.
- Serve spooned over the lobster.

Makes about 1½ cups

SEAFOOD

Chili Garlic Conch

This is a delicious Szechwan method of cooking conch (lambie).
Be careful not to overcook the conch or it could become tough.
Serve the dish with plain rice.

- **1 lb conch, skin removed, tenderized and cut into strips (see page 63)**
- **1 tsp fresh lime juice**
- **4 tbs vegetable oil**
- **¼ cup cornstarch**
- **1 tbs finely minced garlic**
- **1 tbs minced ginger**
- **chopped chives**

FOR THE MARINADE
- **¼ tsp salt**
- **2 tsp cooking wine or water**
- **1 tsp sesame oil**
- **2 tbs soy sauce**
- **1 tsp chopped ginger**
- **1 tsp garlic**

FOR THE SAUCE
- **1 tbs Chinese chili garlic sauce**
- **1 tbs soy sauce**
- **1 tbs oyster sauce**
- **1 tsp sugar**
- **¼ cup water**
- **½ tsp cornstarch**

- Wash conch then pour on the lime juice. Rinse again, then drain.
- Mix the marinade ingredients and toss conch in marinade. Let stand for 20 minutes.
- Heat a wok until hot and add 3 tablespoons of the oil. Dredge conch in cornstarch, then fry in the oil for about 1 minute. Remove and drain.
- Combine the sauce ingredients and set aside.
- Clean wok and heat the remaining oil. Add the minced garlic and ginger and stir-fry until fragrant.
- Add sauce and stir-fry for a few seconds. Add conch, stir until sauce thickens and remove to a platter.
- Sprinkle with chopped chives.

Serves 4

SEAFOOD

Coconut Curried Fish with Lemongrass & Hot Peppers

The combination of lemongrass with coconut milk is very exotic and delicious. Lemongrass is also called 'fever grass' on the islands. Here the grassy or green leafy tops are steeped in hot water and drunk as tea to relieve the symptoms of fever and cold. For culinary purposes the thick woody stalks are used.

- **1 lb fresh fish fillets (carite or king fish), cut into 4 portions**
- **1 tbs minced chives, plus 1 tbs finely chopped chives, white and green portions**
- **½ tbs minced garlic**
- **1 tbs vegetable oil**
- **1 onion, chopped**
- **1 red Congo pepper, seeded and cut into strips**
- **1 stalk fresh lemongrass (fever grass), thinly sliced**
- **½ cup coconut milk**
- **2 tbs curry powder**
- **½ tsp fresh lime juice**

- Clean and wash the fish fillets. Sprinkle lightly with salt and freshly ground black pepper, and rub on the minced chives and garlic.
- Heat the oil in a medium sauté pan and add the onion, chopped chives, hot pepper and lemongrass. Sauté until fragrant, about 3 minutes.
- Mix the coconut milk with the curry powder. Add to pan and bring to a boil. Reduce heat and simmer for about 2–3 minutes.
- Add the fish fillets to the pan and cook for about 4 minutes on each side, basting with the sauce.
- Remove from heat, adjust seasoning, sprinkle on lime juice and serve immediately.

Serves 4

For a lighter dish
Use less coconut milk and substitute stock, or use low fat coconut milk.

Oven Baked Fillets
with Fresh Herbs

- **1 tbs minced chives**
- **½ tbs fresh French thyme**
- **2 garlic cloves, minced**
- **2 tbs olive oil**
- **4 x 6 oz fresh fish fillets**
- **½ lime**

- Combine the chives, thyme, garlic, olive oil, and salt and freshly ground black pepper. Rub onto the fish and let marinate for 20 minutes.
- Preheat oven to 375ºF
- Place fillets in a shallow baking dish and bake for about 4 minutes per side. Remove when fish flakes easily and is opaque.
- Serve with a light squeeze of lime over the fish.

Serves 4

Pasta with Peanut, Cilantro & Ginger Flavored Shrimp

- **½ lb shell or bowtie pasta**
- **1 lb shrimp, seasoned with minced garlic and salt and grilled**
- **1 cup chopped chives**

FOR THE SAUCE
- **4 garlic cloves**
- **2 inch piece of ginger, peeled**
- **1 cup cilantro (chadon beni) leaves**
- **3 tbs fresh lime juice**
- **¼ cup peanut butter**
- **¼ cup peanuts**
- **¼ cup sunflower oil**
- **1 tsp sesame oil**
- **1 tsp dried pepper**

- Place all the ingredients for the sauce into a blender or food processor and blend until smooth.
- Boil the pasta and drain.
- Toss with the shrimp, then mix with the sauce and sprinkle with chives.

Serves 4

Jerked Fish in Banana Leaves with Coconut Lemongrass Sauce

- **6 fish steaks (king fish), 1 inch thick**
- **6 banana leaves, 10 x 10 inches, steamed for about 10 minutes to soften**

FOR THE JERK SEASONING

- **3 tbs allspice berries, ground**
- **2 hot peppers (habanero, Congo or scotch bonnet) or more to taste, seeded and chopped**
- **8 blades of chives, white and green parts**
- **1 large onion, chopped**
- **8 garlic cloves**
- **2 inch piece of ginger**
- **⅓ cup fresh thyme**
- **½ tsp grated nutmeg**
- **1 tsp ground cinnamon**
- **½ tbs freshly ground black pepper**
- **2 tbs fresh lime juice**
- **⅓ cup vegetable oil**

FOR THE COCONUT LEMONGRASS SAUCE

- **1 tbs vegetable oil**
- **2 garlic cloves, minced**
- **2 stalks fresh lemongrass (fever grass), thinly sliced**
- **¾ cup fresh coconut milk**

- To make the jerk seasoning: in a blender or food processor process all the ingredients to a smooth paste.
- Rub 1 teaspoon of jerk onto each fish steak, and let marinate for 10 minutes.
- Meanwhile, make the coconut lemongrass sauce: heat the oil in a medium sauté pan. Add the garlic and lemongrass and sauté until fragrant, about 1 minute. Add the coconut milk to the pan and bring to a boil. Reduce the heat and simmer for about 10 minutes until sauce is slightly reduced. Season with salt and freshly ground black pepper.
- Wrap each fish steak in a banana leaf.
- Assemble the steamer, place fish in steamer and steam for about 10–15 minutes until it flakes easily and is opaque.
- Unwrap, place fish onto plate and serve with the coconut lemongrass sauce.

Serves 4–6

SEAFOOD

94

SEAFOOD

Grilled Shrimp
with Rum Chili Glaze

- **25 large shrimp,
  peeled and deveined, tails intact**
- **1 tbs minced garlic**

FOR THE GLAZE
- **¼ cup unsalted butter**
- **1 onion, grated**
- **2 tbs brown sugar**
- **¼ cup dark rum**
- **⅛ tsp allspice powder**
- **½ tsp chili powder**
- **juice of 1 large lime**
- **1 tsp chopped hot pepper
  (optional)**

- Marinate the shrimp in the garlic, with salt and freshly ground black pepper for about 20 minutes.
- Meanwhile make the glaze: melt the butter in a small saucepan, add the onion and sauté until fragrant, about 2–3 minutes, being careful not to brown or burn the onion.
- Add the brown sugar, rum, allspice, chili powder, lime juice and pepper, if using. Stir well, cook until bubbling, then reduce heat, cover, and simmer for 15 minutes stirring occasionally. The mixture will thicken. Remove from the heat.
- Preheat broiler or grill.
- Thread the shrimp onto skewers (if using wooden skewers, soak in water for 1 hour before using).
- Grill the shrimp until pink and curled, about 3 minutes each side.
- Remove and brush generously with the glaze. Return to grill for a few minutes, turn, brush other side with glaze.
- Serve hot with additional glaze if desired.

Serves 4

Fricassee of Conch

This is a French Caribbean speciality,
an adaptation of a meal I enjoyed on the island of Martinique.

- **2 lb conch, cleaned,
  tenderized and chopped
  (see page 63)**
- **1 tbs chopped garlic**
- **2 tbs vegetable oil**
- **2 onions, chopped**
- **1 green bell pepper,
  seeded and chopped**
- **2 red pimento peppers,
  seeded and chopped**
- **1 hot pepper, seeded and chopped**
- **4 tomatoes, chopped**
- **¼ tsp allspice powder**
- **⅓ cup chopped parsley**
- **⅓ cup chopped Spanish thyme**
- **¼ cup chopped chives**

- Season the conch with ½ tablespoon of garlic, and salt and freshly ground black pepper.
- Heat 1 tablespoon of the oil, add the conch and quickly stir-fry for a few minutes. Remove the conch.
- Heat the remaining oil in a pot, add the remaining garlic, the onions and peppers and stir and fry until fragrant. Add tomatoes and allspice together with about ¼ cup water and cook for about 6–8 minutes more, covered, on a low heat.
- Return the conch to the pot, add herbs, and stir. Cover and cook for about 6 minutes more. Serve hot.

Serves 4

SEAFOOD

Plantain-crusted Fish

This is a Spanish Caribbean dish where the plantain chips act as the crumb covering before frying – very flavorful and delicious!

- **4 fish fillets (carite, kingfish, white salmon)**
- **1 tsp minced garlic**
- **1 tbs minced chives**
- **1 tsp French thyme**
- **2 cups crushed plantain chips**
- **flour**
- **1 egg, beaten**
- **vegetable oil for frying**

- Season the fish fillets with the garlic, fresh herbs, and salt and freshly ground black pepper.
- Place the crushed plantain chips on a plate. Place some flour on another plate. Pour the beaten egg into a shallow dish.
- Dip the fish fillets into the flour, then into the egg, then into the crushed plantain chips.
- Fry in hot oil and serve immediately.
- Serve with spicy tomato salsa (page 311) or tartar sauce.

Serves 4

SEAFOOD

Stuffed Flying Fish

- **10 flying fish fillets**
- **juice of 1 lime**
- **1 tbs minced chives**
- **1 tsp French thyme**
- **1 tsp ground garlic**
- **2 tbs olive oil**
- **2 tbs chopped cilantro (chadon beni)**
- **2 cups good quality tomato sauce**
- **grated cheese (optional)**

FOR THE STUFFING
- **2 tbs vegetable oil**
- **1 onion, finely chopped**
- **2 garlic cloves, minced**
- **2 pimento peppers, seeded and chopped**
- **1 hot pepper, seeded and chopped**
- **2 tbs French thyme**
- **⅓ cup finely chopped chives**
- **½ lb crab meat**
- **1 cup bread crumbs**
- **stock if necessary**

• To make the stuffing: heat the oil and add the onion, garlic, peppers, thyme and chives. Cook until fragrant and soft, about 6 minutes, then add the crab and stir well. Add the bread crumbs just to bind and bring together, about ½ cup at a time. If the mixture seems a little dry, add some stock. Add salt to taste. Leave to cool.

• Preheat oven to 375°F.

• Soak the fish in the lime juice with some salt for 5 minutes. Drain and rinse.

• Rub the fish with the chives, thyme, garlic and olive oil and sprinkle with salt. Make sure that you stuff the slits with the herbs.

• Place the fish skin side down in a large shallow baking dish, spoon stuffing onto each fillet and press down.

• Sprinkle with cilantro, spoon tomato sauce over and top with grated cheese if desired.

• Bake in the oven for 15 minutes.

Serves 6

Note
Most flying fish are sold cleaned, boned and frozen in packs of five. They are ready to prepare, with slits already there from the boning process.

Crab & Shrimp Pastelles

Pastelles are traditionally served at Christmas time and are usually stuffed with beef or chicken.
Here, the seafood makes a healthy change!

- **twelve 9 inch square pieces of prepared fig leaves (see method)**

FOR THE FILLING
- **½ lb shrimp**
- **1 cup chopped chives**
- **¼ cup chopped fresh Spanish thyme**
- **½ lb crab meat**
- **4 tbs olive oil**
- **3 onions, finely chopped**
- **4 garlic cloves, chopped**
- **2 pimento peppers, seeded and chopped**
- **½ Congo pepper, seeded and chopped (optional)**
- **¼ cup tomato sauce**
- **⅓ cup raisins**
- **2 tbs capers**
- **2 tbs stuffed olives, sliced**
- **1 tsp salt**
- **1 tsp freshly ground black pepper**
- **½ cup chopped parsley**

FOR THE CORNMEAL DOUGH
- **2 cups yellow cornmeal**
- **½ cup butter**
- **1¼ tsp salt**
- **3 cups warm water**

- To prepare fig leaves, steam them in a large pot of boiling water for 10 minutes until they become pliable and soft. Alternatively, they may be softened by waving them over an open flame.
- To make the filling: combine the shrimp with 1 tablespoon chopped chives and ½ tablespoon thyme.

Combine the crab meat with 1 tablespoon chopped chives and ½ tablespoon thyme.
- Heat the olive oil in a large sauté pan. Add the onion and garlic and sauté until fragrant. Add the peppers and cook until fragrant.
- Add the shrimp and sauté for about 3–4 minutes, remove and chop finely. Return to the pan with the crab meat.
- Add the tomato sauce together with the remaining thyme and chives. Cover and simmer for about 15 minutes.
- Add the raisins, capers and olives and stir to combine. Cook for about 5 minutes more, then add the salt and pepper. Add the parsley and stir to combine. Remove from heat and leave to cool.
- To make the dough: in a food processor or by hand, combine the cornmeal with the butter and salt. Add the water and process to make a soft, pliable dough. Divide the dough into 12 balls and cover with a damp cloth to prevent drying.
- Place one piece of dough on a greased fig leaf, and press to an 8 inch width. Spoon 2 tablespoons of the filling onto the middle of the dough and fold and seal the pastelle. Wrap in the fig leaf and tie into a neat package. Repeat with the remaining dough.
- Steam the pastelles for 45 minutes until cooked.

Makes 12

SEAFOOD

Maracas Shark & Float with Chadon Beni Pesto

A visit to Trinidad's famous Maracas beach will reveal many food huts all selling the hearty fish sandwich called 'shark and bake'. Here's my version, topped with a delightful chadon beni, or cilantro, pesto.

- 1 lb shark fillets
- 1 tsp minced chives
- 1 tbs minced cilantro (chadon beni)
- 2 garlic cloves, minced
- juice of 1 lime
- vegetable oil for frying
- flour

FOR THE FLOATS
- 4 cups flour
- 2 tsp instant yeast
- 1 tsp salt
- 1 tbs sugar
- 1 tbs shortening
- vegetable oil for deep frying

- Wash shark, cut into 4 oz portions, and season with the herbs, garlic, lime juice, and salt and freshly ground black pepper. Marinate for 30 minutes.
- To make the floats: combine the flour with the yeast, salt and sugar. Rub in the shortening until the mixture resembles fine crumbs. Add enough warm water to make a soft dough.
- Knead for 5 minutes, form into a smooth ball, cover, and leave for 30 minutes until doubled in size.
- Form the dough into 8 balls. Let rise again for 15 minutes.
- Flatten the balls into 4 inch rounds.
- Heat oil in a deep frying pan and deep fry the floats until they actually float to the top of the oil. Turn and fry until golden. Drain and keep warm while frying the fish.
- Heat the oil in a frying pan, dredge the fish in flour and fry until golden.
- Serve the shark topped with chadon beni pesto (page 311) together with the floats.

Serves 4

Salt Cod Potato Bake

Salted fish is used quite a bit in Caribbean cooking.
We make fish salads with it, stew it with tomatoes and onions,
and also use it in fritters. Here it makes a different and delicious
casserole with potato. Serve this as a light lunch,
brunch or hearty breakfast dish.

- 4 tbs butter
- 3 tbs flour
- 3 cups milk
- 1 large onion, chopped finely
- 2 garlic cloves, chopped finely
- 4 leaves cilantro (chadon beni)
- 4 leaves Spanish thyme
- ¼ tsp grated nutmeg
- 1½ cups soaked and stripped salt cod
- 2 cups cubed boiled potatoes
- 2 hard-boiled eggs, diced
- 1 cup bread crumbs

- Preheat oven to 375ºF.
- Melt the butter, add the flour and stir until smooth and liquid. Add the milk and cook until thick.
- Add the onion, garlic, herbs and nutmeg. Stir, and add the salt fish, potato and eggs. Stir gently.
- Spoon into an ovenproof dish and sprinkle with the bread crumbs. Bake for 30 minutes.

Serves 4–6

Stewed Salt Fish with Cassava

- ½ lb salt cod
- juice of 1 lime
- ¼ cup olive oil
- 1 lb onions, sliced
- 1 pimento pepper, seeded and chopped
- 1 hot pepper, seeded and chopped (optional)
- 2 garlic cloves, chopped
- 1 lb tomatoes, chopped
- cassava, to serve

- The night before, soak the cod in plenty of cold water together with the lime juice, changing the water three times.
- When ready to cook, squeeze out excess water and remove any bones and skin. Cut the fish into strips.
- Heat the oil in a sauté pan and add the onions, pepper and garlic. Cook until fragrant, about 3–5 minutes.
- Add the salt fish, combine, and cook for about 4 minutes, then add the tomatoes and season with freshly ground black pepper if desired. Cover and simmer for 15 minutes.
- Serve hot with boiled cassava.

Serves 4–6

Caribbean
Seafood Quiche

- milk
- 3 eggs, beaten
- 1 cup grated cheese
- 1 lb small shrimp, peeled and deveined
- 1 tbs minced chives plus ½ cup chopped chives
- 1 tbs butter or olive oil
- 1 small onion, chopped
- 1 tsp minced garlic
- 1 prebaked pie crust
- 2 tbs chopped cilantro (chadon beni)

- Preheat oven to 350ºF.
- Add enough milk to the beaten eggs to make a mixture of about 1½ cups. Add the cheese and stir.
- Rub the shrimp with the minced chives.
- Heat the butter or oil in a frying pan, add the onion and garlic, and sauté until translucent and fragrant. Add the shrimp and sauté until pink, then add the chopped chives and season with salt and freshly ground black pepper.
- Place the shrimp mixture into the pie crust, pour the milk and egg mixture over the shrimp, and sprinkle with cilantro.
- Bake for 30 minutes until firm.
- Leave to cool a little before slicing.

Serves 4–6

Lime &
Garlic Grilled Shrimp

- ¼ cup fresh lime juice
- ⅓ cup vegetable or olive oil
- ¼ cup finely chopped parsley
- 4 garlic cloves, minced
- 2 tsp grated lime zest
- 24 large shrimp,
  peeled and deveined

• In a mixing bowl combine the lime juice, oil, parsley, garlic, lime zest, and salt and freshly ground black pepper. Place the shrimp in the marinade and toss. Cover and refrigerate for 30 minutes.
• Thread the shrimp onto a metal skewer or a wooden skewer that has been soaked in water for 30 minutes.
• Cook the shrimp on a greased grill over medium hot coals or broil, brushing often with the marinade. Cook for 2 minutes per side or until firm to the touch.

Serves 8

SEAFOOD

Smoked Fish Oiled Down

An oiled down, also called run down on some islands, is a method of cooking provisions in coconut milk until all the milk is absorbed by the provisions and they thereby become soft and creamy. This oiled down is infused with the flavors of peppers, fresh herbs and smoked fish.

- ¼ lb salt fish
- ¼ lb smoked herring
- juice of 1 lime
- 3 lb assorted provisions or breadfruit (see page 157)
- 2 tbs vegetable oil
- 1 cup chopped onion
- 4 garlic cloves, chopped
- 1 Congo pepper, seeded and chopped, plus 1 whole Congo pepper (optional)
- 1 large pimento pepper, seeded and chopped
- ¾ cup chopped fresh chives, green and white portion
- 2 tbs chopped fresh thyme
- 3 cups fresh coconut milk
- 1 tsp salt

- Soak the fish with the lime for about 30 minutes. Drain and flake.
- Peel and cut the provisions into 2 inch pieces.
- Heat the oil in a large heavy frying pan and add the onion, garlic, chopped peppers, chives and thyme. Sauté until fragrant, about 4 minutes. Add the fish and cook for a few minutes more.
- Add the coconut milk and bring mixture to a boil. Lower the heat and add the provisions. Drop in the whole Congo pepper at this point, if using.
- Cover mixture and simmer for about 25–30 minutes until all the coconut milk has been absorbed and the provisions are cooked and tender. There should be only a small amount of coconut oil at the bottom of the pan when the provisions are cooked. Season with the salt.

Serves 6–8

Curried Shrimp with Lemongrass

- **1½ lb large shrimp, peeled and deveined**
- **2 tsp minced garlic**
- **1 heaped tbs curry powder**
- **½ cup coconut milk**
- **1 tbs vegetable oil**
- **1 stalk lemongrass, thinly sliced**
- **½ hot pepper, seeded and chopped**
- **2 tbs chopped cilantro (chadon beni)**

- Combine the shrimp with the garlic and set aside.
- Combine the curry powder with the coconut milk.
- Heat the oil in a sauté pan. Add the lemongrass to the pan with the hot pepper. Sauté until fragrant, add the curry powder mixture and cook until thick.
- Add the shrimp and cook until pink and curled, adding only small amounts of water to prevent sticking.
- Add salt and freshly ground black pepper to taste. Sprinkle with cilantro and serve.

Serves 4

For a lighter dish
Use milk in place of coconut milk.

SEAFOOD

Breaded Sardines with Spicy Salsa

- **1 lb fresh sardines, cleaned and washed in lime juice**
- **2 tsp minced chives**
- **1 tsp ground garlic plus 2 garlic cloves, minced**
- **1 cup flour**
- **1 egg, beaten**
- **1 cup toasted bread crumbs**
- **oil for frying**
- **fresh lime or lemon juice**

- Combine the sardines with the minced chives and ground and minced garlic, and season to taste with salt and freshly ground black pepper.
- Season the flour with salt and freshly ground black pepper.
- Dredge the sardines in the flour, dip into beaten egg and coat with crumbs.
- Heat the oil in a frying pan or wok. Drop the sardines into the hot oil and fry until golden. Remove and drain.
- Squeeze some lime juice over the sardines and serve with spicy tomato salsa (page 311).

Serves 4–6 as an appetizer

Curried Fish with Coconut Chutney

- **2 lb fresh fish fillets**
- **½ tbs minced chives**
- **2 garlic cloves, minced**
- **2 tbs vegetable oil**
- **1 onion, thinly sliced**
- **½ hot pepper, seeded and chopped**
- **2 tbs light curry powder mixed with ¼ cup water**
- **1 tbs tamarind paste or purée**
- **½ lime**

- Season fish with the chives, garlic, and salt and freshly ground black pepper.
- Heat the oil in a sauté pan. Add the onion and hot pepper and cook until transparent. Add the curry mixture and cook until almost dry.
- Gently add the fish, and cook for a few minutes, then turn, cover and simmer, adding a little water only if necessary to prevent sticking. Add the tamarind paste.
- Cook, basting frequently, until the fish is ready, about 20 minutes.
- Squeeze lime over and serve hot with coconut chutney.

Serves 4

Coconut Chutney

- **1 coconut, cracked and meat removed in large pieces**
- **1 hot pepper, seeded and chopped**
- **4 garlic cloves**
- **1 small onion**
- **2 sprigs of cilantro (chadon beni)**

- Wash and dry the coconut meat Roast over an open flame until browned on all sides.
- Grate or blend in a blender with the pepper, garlic, onion and cilantro.
- Add salt to taste.

Serves 4

Fish & Bok Choy Gratin

My mother always prepared this dish for us when we were growing up. Today it still tops my list of favorite fish dishes!

- 1½ lb fish fillets
- 2 garlic cloves, minced
- 2 tbs minced chives
- 1 tsp fresh thyme
- 1 tbs vegetable oil
- 1 onion, sliced
- 1 small bunch bok choy, chopped

FOR THE SAUCE
- 3 tbs butter
- 3 tbs flour
- 1 cup milk

FOR THE GRATIN
- ⅓ cup bread crumbs
- 1 tbs olive oil
- ⅓ cup grated cheese

• Season the fish with the garlic, herbs, salt and freshly ground black pepper.

• Bring about 2 cups water to a boil and poach fish in the water for 10 minutes. Drain, flake fish and reserve water, about 1 cup.

• Heat the oil in a sauté pan and add the onion. Add the bok choy and lightly sauté until wilted, about 3–5 minutes. Remove and set aside.

• To make the sauce: melt the butter in a heavy saucepan, add the flour and cook until cream-like in consistency. Add the milk and the reserved cooking water and stir until thick and free of any lumps. Add salt to taste.

• Preheat oven to 375ºF.

• Combine all the gratin ingredients.

• Place the flaked fish in a greased casserole dish, top with bok choy and then with sauce. Sprinkle with the gratin and bake for 20–30 minutes until hot and bubbly.

Serves 4

Grilled Marinated Fish with Roasted Habanero Tomato Salsa

- 1 tsp vegetable oil
- 1 tbs grated fresh ginger
- 2 garlic cloves, minced
- 1 tsp roasted ground coriander
- 4 fish fillets (mahi mahi or king fish), each weighing 5–6 oz
- cilantro to garnish (optional)

FOR THE SALSA
- 4 ripe tomatoes
- 1 green habanero pepper (or any hot pepper), roasted, seeded and chopped
- 1½ tbs fresh lime juice
- 2 large garlic cloves, minced
- 2 tsp olive oil
- 1 tbs coriander seeds, toasted and ground
- ½ tsp salt
- 1 tsp freshly ground black pepper
- ¼ cup finely chopped cilantro (chadon beni)

- Mix the vegetable oil with the grated ginger and minced garlic. Stir in the ground coriander and add salt and freshly ground black pepper to taste.
- Wash fish and pat dry. Spread the marinade over both sides, cover and refrigerate for 20–30 minutes.
- Meanwhile make the salsa: peel, seed and chop the tomatoes. Add the roasted pepper, lime juice, garlic, oil and ground coriander. Season to taste with the salt and pepper and set aside.
- Preheat broiler or grill, and broil fish for about 3–5 minutes on each side.
- Add the cilantro to the salsa just before serving.
- Serve the fish topped with the salsa. Sprinkle with fresh cilantro if desired.

Serves 4

Stuffed Flying Fish with Spicy Tomato Cilantro Sauce

- **2 packages flying fish fillets (about 10)**
- **1 tsp minced garlic**
- **2 tbs fresh herb seasoning (see opposite)**
- **juice of 1 lime**

FOR THE STUFFING
- **6 black dried Chinese mushrooms (soaked in warm water for 30 minutes)**
- **2 tbs vegetable oil**
- **2 onions, finely chopped**
- **2 tsp chopped garlic**
- **4 pimento peppers, seeded and chopped**
- **½ hot pepper, seeded and chopped**
- **1 green bell pepper, seeded and chopped**
- **⅔ cup chopped chives**
- **2 tbs chopped celery**
- **⅔ cup soft bread crumbs**
- **⅔ cup chopped parsley**

FOR THE SAUCE
- **½ tbs vegetable oil**
- **1 small onion, finely chopped**
- **4 garlic cloves, minced**
- **14 oz can whole tomatoes**
- **pinch of sugar**
- **¼ cup chopped cilantro (chadon beni)**

- Wash the fish fillets and marinate in salt, freshly ground black pepper, the garlic and seasoning paste. Rub and sprinkle with lime juice.
- Meanwhile, prepare the stuffing and the sauce. To make the stuffing: drain the mushrooms, reserving the soaking water. Remove the stems, discard, and chop the mushrooms.
- Heat the oil in a sauté pan and add the onion, garlic and peppers. Cook until fragrant, then add the mushrooms and sauté for a few minutes more.
- Add the chives and celery and cook until all the ingredients are tender, about 5 minutes.
- Add the bread crumbs and stir to combine. If the mixture seems dry then add a little of the mushroom water. Add the parsley and combine. Remove from heat and leave to cool.

- To make the sauce: heat the oil in a saucepan, add the onion and garlic, and stir and fry until tender and fragrant, about 3–5 minutes. Add the tomatoes, sugar, and salt and freshly ground black pepper.
- Cover, and simmer for 30–40 minutes until the tomatoes have lost their acidity and the sauce is thick. Add the cilantro, remove from heat and leave to cool.
- Preheat oven to 375ºF.
- Place a little sauce at the bottom of a greased casserole dish.
- Place a flying fish fillet skin side down onto a flat surface, spread about 1–2 tablespoons of stuffing onto the fillet, spread and roll up. Hold the ends together with a toothpick. Place fish into casserole dish and repeat with the remaining fillets.
- Spoon the rest of the sauce over the fish and bake for 15 minutes until bubbling and fillets are tender.

Serves 4–6

Fresh Herb Seasoning

- **2 large bunches of chives plus 12 blades of chives (green and white parts)**
- **1 bunch of fresh French thyme**
- **6 garlic cloves**
- **a few sprigs of fresh oregano or Portuguese thyme**
- **white vinegar (see method**)

- Purée all the ingredients in a blender or food processor. Add some white vinegar, if needed, to bring it to a paste-like consistency.

Creamy Pesto Shrimp

- **2 lb medium shrimp, peeled and deveined**
- **8 garlic cloves, minced, plus ½ tbs minced garlic**
- **2 tbs olive oil**
- **2 tbs flour**
- **1½ cups milk**

FOR THE PESTO
- **1 cup fresh basil leaves**
- **2–4 garlic cloves**
- **¼ cup olive oil**

TO SERVE
- **linguine or spaghetti**
- **½ cup chopped parsley**
- **Parmesan cheese (optional)**

- Season the shrimp with ½ tablespoon minced garlic, salt and freshly ground black pepper. Set aside.
- To make the pesto: purée the basil and garlic then add the olive oil.
- Heat the oil in a saucepan, add the garlic and cook without browning until fragrant.
- Add the flour and cook until smooth, then add the milk and stir until smooth. Cook until sauce is quite thick. Season with salt and freshly ground black pepper.
- Add shrimp to the sauce. Cook until bubbling, then cover and simmer just until the shrimp are pink and curled (the shrimp will water a bit), about 3–5 minutes.
- Add the pesto, increase the heat and cook a few minutes more until the sauce thickens again.
- Remove and serve immediately over a bed of linguine or spaghetti. Sprinkle with parsley and Parmesan cheese if desired.

Serves 4

SEAFOOD

Caribbean Pasta with Mussels & Shrimp

- **1 lb medium shrimp, peeled and deveined**
- **½ cup chopped chives plus 1 tbs minced chives**
- **5 garlic cloves, finely chopped, plus 1 tbs ground garlic and 1 tsp minced garlic**
- **12–15 mussels on the half shell**
- **1 lemon**
- **1 tbs butter**
- **1 large onion, minced**
- **½ cup white wine or broth**
- **2 tbs olive oil**
- **1 rounded tsp chili powder**
- **½ tsp saffron powder**
- **4 small tomatoes, seeded and chopped**
- **½ lb linguine pasta, boiled and drained**
- **salt and freshly ground black pepper**
- **½ cup chopped parsley**
- **½ cup chopped mint**

- Marinate the shrimp in the minced chives, ground garlic, salt and freshly ground black pepper. Refrigerate until ready for use.
- Combine the mussels with the minced garlic and squeeze ½ lemon over.
- Melt the butter in a heavy saucepan, add the minced onion and sauté until fragrant. Add the mussels, toss, and add the wine or broth. Cover and simmer for 6–8 minutes. Remove from heat and set aside.
- Heat the oil in a large sauté pan, add the chopped garlic and chives, and sauté for a few seconds without allowing the garlic to brown. Add the shrimp and turn to combine.
- Add the chili powder and saffron powder and stir to coat shrimp thoroughly. Add the chopped tomatoes, salt and freshly ground black pepper and continue turning. Cook for a few minutes, then add the mussels with all their pan juices.
- Cover, lower heat, and cook for another 3–4 minutes.
- Add linguine to the pan, toss, and squeeze ½ lemon over. Sprinkle with chopped herbs and serve at once.

Serves 4

Stuffed Open-faced Fish Fillets

- **1 tbs olive oil**
- **1 tsp minced garlic**
- **1 tsp minced chives**
- **½ tsp salt and freshly ground black pepper**
- **1½ lb fish fillets (such as snapper), cut into portion sizes**

FOR THE STUFFING
- **1 tbs vegetable oil**
- **1 onion, chopped**
- **1 tbs chopped chives**
- **1 tsp minced garlic**
- **⅓ cup chopped red sweet pepper**
- **6–8 small shrimp, chopped**
- **½ cup soft bread crumbs**
- **⅓ cup grated Parmesan cheese**
- **⅓ cup chopped parsley**

• Combine the olive oil with the garlic, chives, salt and pepper. Rub onto fish and let marinate for 20 minutes.
• To make the stuffing: heat the vegetable oil in a sauté pan. Add the onion, chives, garlic, pepper and shrimp. Sauté for 5 minutes, then add the bread crumbs and salt and freshly ground black pepper to taste.
• Add the cheese and 1 tablespoon of water, and stir to bring the stuffing together (add more water if necessary). Add the parsley, taste and adjust seasonings. Leave to cool.
• Preheat broiler or grill.
• Place fish fillets onto a baking tray and place under broiler for 3 minutes. Remove fish from broiler.
• Turn fish over. Spoon stuffing onto fillets and replace under broiler.
• Broil for another 4 minutes until the fish is opaque and flakes easily. Remove and serve at once.

Serves 4

SEAFOOD

Roasted Fish with Sautéed Vegetables

- **6 fish fillets (preferably salmon or carite), each weighing 6 oz**
- **2 tbs minced chives**
- **1 tsp thyme**
- **2 garlic cloves, minced**
- **1 tbs olive oil**
- **1 lime, sliced**

FOR THE VEGETABLES
- **2 tbs olive oil**
- **1 sprig of French thyme or 2 leaves Spanish thyme**
- **2 garlic cloves, chopped**
- **1 onion, chopped**
- **1 pimento pepper, seeded and chopped**
- **⅓ cup chopped red bell pepper**
- **2 ripe tomatoes, chopped**

- Marinate the fish in the herbs, garlic, olive oil, salt and freshly milled black pepper. Cover and refrigerate for about 20 minutes.
- Preheat oven to 400ºF.
- To prepare the vegetables: heat a sauté pan and add the oil. When hot, add the sprig of French thyme, if using, the garlic, onion and peppers. Sauté for about 3–4 minutes. Add the Spanish thyme, if using, and the tomatoes, and cook for just 2 minutes more. Season to taste with salt and freshly ground black pepper.
- Place the marinated fish into a lightly greased casserole dish and top with the cooked vegetables. Place in the hot oven and cook for about 10 minutes, until the fish is opaque and flakes easily.
- Remove and serve at once with slices of lime.

Serves 6

Curried Conch

- **1 lb conch,
  skin removed, tenderized
  and chopped (see page 63)**
- **1 lime**
- **2 tbs minced chives**
- **1 tsp minced garlic**
- **2 tbs vegetable oil**
- **2 small onions, sliced**
- **1½ tbs curry powder mixed
  with ¼ cup water**
- **1 hot pepper, seeded and chopped**
- **½ cup coconut milk (optional)**
- **1 tbs cilantro (chadon beni)**

• Finish preparing the conch by washing in limed water. Add the chives and garlic. Let stand for 30 minutes.

• Heat the oil in a frying pan and add the onions. Sauté until almost brown, then add the curry paste and stir and fry until all the water has evaporated. Add the conch and hot pepper, stir well. Add the coconut milk, if using, and stir.

• Cook for a few minutes uncovered, then cover and cook on a low heat for about 20 minutes, adding a small amount of water at a time, if necessary, to prevent sticking.

• Sprinkle with cilantro and serve with additional lime if desired.

Serves 4

SEAFOOD

Oven-fried Fish Fillets

- **1 lb fresh fish fillets, cut into 4 oz portions**
- **1 tsp minced chives**
- **2 garlic cloves, ground**
- **1 cup cornmeal**
- **1 tsp chili powder**
- **½ cup fine bread crumbs**
- **1 tsp salt**
- **½ tsp freshly ground black pepper**
- **¾ cup all-purpose flour**
- **1 tsp baking powder**
- **¼ tsp baking soda**
- **1 egg white**
- **¾ cup milk, curdled with 1 tbs lime juice**

- Preheat oven to 375°F.
- Season the fish with the chives, garlic, salt and freshly ground black pepper and set aside.
- On a plate, combine the cornmeal with the chili powder and set aside.
- On another plate, season the bread crumbs with the salt and pepper and set aside.
- Combine the flour with the baking powder and soda and season with salt and pepper.
- Beat the egg white until soft, then add the milk and the flour mixture.
- Dredge fish in bread crumbs, then in the batter mixture, then in cornmeal.
- Place on a greased baking dish and bake for about 12–15 minutes until the fish flakes easily.

Serves 4

Caribbean Fish & Pasta

- **1 lb firm fleshed fish,
  cut into cubes**
- **2 garlic cloves, minced**
- **1 tbs minced chives**
- **1 tbs olive oil**
- **1 onion, sliced**
- **1 bell pepper, cut into strips**
- **⅓ cup chopped cilantro
  (chadon beni)**
- **½ lb spaghetti,
  boiled and drained**
- **¼ cup chopped parsley**
- **½ lime**

- Rub the fish with the garlic, chives, salt and freshly ground black pepper and marinate for about 30 minutes.
- Heat the oil in a large frying pan and add the onion and pepper. Fry until fragrant and just tender. Add the fish and gently toss to combine. Cook for about 10 minutes, turning occasionally, until fish is tender. Add the cilantro, taste and adjust seasoning.
- Remove from pan, toss with the cooked pasta and sprinkle with parsley.
- Squeeze lime over and serve.

Serves 4

Seafood Frittata

- **1 tbs olive oil**
- **½ cup chopped red bell pepper**
- **1 onion, chopped**
- **⅓ cup chopped chives**
- **4 eggs, beaten**
- **2 tomatoes, sliced**
- **1 cup mixed seafood (shrimp or crab or both), lightly steamed**
- **½ cup grated cheese**
- **2 tbs chopped parsley**

- Preheat broiler or grill.
- Heat the oil in a non-stick ovenproof frying pan and add the pepper, onion and chives. Flash fry for a few seconds and remove from the pan.
- Pour the beaten eggs into the pan and sprinkle on the sautéed onion mixture. Arrange the tomatoes, then the seafood over the top, and sprinkle with the cheese. Season with salt and freshly ground black pepper.
- Place under broiler for 5 minutes or more, until the frittata is puffed and golden.
- Remove and sprinkle with parsley.

Serves 4–6

Breakfast Sardines with Fresh Herbs

This is a great way to use canned sardines.
They make wonderful breakfast sandwiches when served with large
crusty rolls. Garnish them with hot sauce!

- **1 can water-packed sardines, drained and cleaned**
- **½ tbs fresh lime juice**
- **2 eggs**
- **½ cup chopped chives, white and green portion**
- **⅓ cup chopped cilantro (chadon beni)**
- **1 pimento pepper, seeded and chopped**
- **¼ cup lightly toasted bread crumbs**
- **1 tsp pepper sauce**
- **salt and freshly ground black pepper**
- **1 tbs olive oil**

- Place the sardines into a mixing bowl, crush, and add all the other ingredients except the oil. Mix gently.
- Heat the oil in a frying pan, spoon the mixture into the oil by tablespoons and pan fry until golden. Turn and cook for a few minutes longer, drain and serve.

Makes 8

Fish Baked on Callaloo Leaves

- **1½ lb fresh fish fillets**
- **4 garlic cloves, minced**
- **1 tbs minced chives**
- **1 tbs minced basil plus 6 basil leaves**
- **1 tbs vegetable oil**
- **1 bunch callaloo bush (taro), preferably rolled, tips removed and chopped**
- **¼ cup coconut milk**
- **1 tomato, sliced**
- **1 hot banana pepper, sliced**
- **¼ cup grated Parmesan cheese (optional)**

FOR THE SAUCE
- **2 tbs butter**
- **2 tbs flour**
- **1½ cups milk**
- **½ tsp salt and freshly ground black pepper**
- **pinch of grated nutmeg**

- Rub the fish with half the garlic, the minced chives and basil and marinate for 30 minutes.
- Heat the oil in a sauté pan, add the remaining garlic and cook until fragrant and tender but not brown. Add the callaloo and sauté until wilted. Season with salt and freshly ground black pepper, add the coconut milk, and cover and simmer until tender, about 15 minutes, stirring occasionally.

- To make the sauce: melt the butter in a small saucepan, add the flour and cook to a smooth paste, without browning. Add the milk and stir to remove any lumps. Cook until thick, season with the salt and pepper, and add the nutmeg. Remove from the heat.
- Preheat oven to 350°F.
- Assemble the casserole. Place the cooked callaloo onto the base of a greased ovenproof dish. Spread it evenly, then lay the seasoned fish fillets on top. Place the tomato slices on top of the fish, together with the basil leaves and pepper.
- Pour the sauce over and sprinkle with Parmesan cheese if desired.
- Bake for 15–20 minutes, just until the fish is tender.

Serves 2–4

Note
If the leaves of the callaloo are rolled at the time you buy them, it means the bunch is young and so much better to use.

meats

Meats form an integral part of the Caribbean diet. Our rich stews derive their color from first caramelizing sugar in oil before adding the meat to the pot – a method handed down to us from our African ancestors. All types of meats are enjoyed on the islands: lamb, chicken, oxtail, beef, pork and goat. And they are prepared in a myriad of ways.

Marinating meat is very important in Caribbean cooking. Marinades are made from a combination of ground fresh herbs, usually mixed with vinegar or lime juice, some garlic and a little oil. Some cooks make up a batch at a time, but I prefer to prepare my marinade as I need it–it's fresher and it means you can also vary the herbs for more versatility in flavor. There are some truly traditional recipes for you in this section, like stewed lamb neck slices and stewed oxtail with cinnamon dumplings, and there are some new recipes as well that truly represent the Caribbean, such as split roasted chicken with guava rum glaze, Mexican tamale pie, and grilled lamb with sesame, hoisin and garlic – just to name a few. All are recipes that use local herbs, spices or fruits and are guaranteed to bring the Caribbean right to your dinner plate!

Split Roasted Chicken with Guava Rum Glaze

- **4½ lb chicken, split into two, washed and cleaned**

FOR THE MARINADE
- **2 tbs red wine vinegar**
- **4 garlic cloves, minced**
- **2 tbs fresh oregano, chopped or minced**
- **2 tbs minced chives**
- **1 tsp salt**
- **1 tsp freshly ground black pepper**
- **2 tbs olive oil**

• Combine all the marinade ingredients and rub onto the chicken, taking care to get the marinade under the skin as well. Cover and refrigerate for about 1 hour or overnight.
• Preheat oven to 400ºF.
• Place the chicken on a baking rack, put it in the oven, and cook for about 40 minutes until browned on both sides.
• Baste chicken on both sides with the guava glaze. Cook for another 5 minutes. Once basted, do not leave too long in the oven as the glaze will burn easily.

Serves 4

Guava Rum Glaze

- **2 tbs vegetable oil**
- **2 tsp grated onion**
- **2 tsp minced garlic**
- **1 cup guava paste**
- **2 tbs tomato ketchup**
- **4 tbs white vinegar**
- **2 tsp yellow mustard**
- **1 tbs brown sugar**
- **1 tbs molasses**
- **¾ tsp cumin (geera)**
- **¼ tsp allspice powder**
- **¼ tsp grated nutmeg**
- **4 tbs rum**
- **salt**

• Heat the vegetable oil in a small saucepan and add the onion and garlic. Stir to combine, then add the rest of the ingredients and cook slowly until well combined and smooth. Cook until bubbling, then remove from heat and use to baste the chicken.
• Refrigerate any unused glaze; it will keep for up to 2 weeks.

You can also use this glaze on grilled mahi mahi or kingfish fillets or grilled steak.

Makes about 1 cup

West Indian Curried Chicken with Ginger

- **2 tbs minced chives**
- **1 tbs French thyme, ground**
- **4 garlic cloves, minced, plus 1 tsp chopped garlic**
- **3½ lb chicken, cut into small pieces**
- **1 tbs wine vinegar or lime juice**
- **2 tbs vegetable oil**
- **1 tsp chopped ginger**
- **1 small onion, sliced**
- **1 hot pepper, seeded and chopped**
- **3 tbs curry powder**
- **2 tbs chopped cilantro (chadon beni) (optional)**

- Combine the chives, thyme and minced garlic and marinate the chicken in the herb paste, vinegar, salt and freshly ground black pepper.
- Heat the oil in a large sauté pan or iron pot and add the chopped garlic, ginger and sliced onion. Stir and add the hot pepper. Sauté until fragrant and the onion is tender.
- Combine the curry powder with ¼ cup water. Add the curry paste to the pot and let it cook, stirring well, until most of the water has evaporated.
- Now add the chicken pieces one at a time, making sure you stir well to cover the chicken with the curry.
- Cover the pot and let the chicken release some water. Stir. If chicken appears to be sticking, add just a small amount of water at a time. Continue cooking in this manner for about 30 minutes. Often, when ready, the curry sauce in the pot will seem to be slightly separating from the oil.
- Taste and adjust seasonings. Sprinkle with cilantro if desired and serve.

Serves 4–6

Grilled Lamb with Lime, Garlic & Oregano Mojo

Mojo is a Spanish Caribbean marinade made with citrus juices and spiced up with garlic, fresh herbs and cumin.
You can use mojo with red meats like lamb and steak and also with the dark meat from poultry.

- **2 lb lamb shoulder chops**

FOR THE MOJO
- **1 cup olive oil**
- **1½ cups fresh lime juice**
- **4 tbs ground garlic**
- **1 tsp cumin (geera)**
- **1 tsp salt or more to taste**
- **½ cup chopped fresh Portuguese thyme or oregano**

- To make the mojo: whisk all the ingredients together to make a thick emulsion (you may use a blender here). Pour the mojo onto the lamb chops and marinate for 4 hours.
- Preheat broiler or grill.
- Drain lamb and grill for about 8 minutes per side, depending on the thickness of the meat and the level of doneness you prefer.

Serves 4–6

Grilled Chicken with Orange, Red Onion & Parsley Mojo

- **4½ lb chicken, washed and cleaned and cut into quarters**

FOR THE MOJO
- **¾ cup orange juice**
- **¼ cup fresh lime juice**
- **1 tsp salt**
- **1 red onion, finely chopped**
- **2 garlic cloves, chopped**
- **¼ cup chopped parsley**
- **½ cup olive oil**
- **½ tsp cumin (geera)**

- To make the mojo: place all the ingredients into a blender and process until incorporated. Set about ¼ cup mojo aside.
- Cover the chicken in the remaining mojo and marinate for 4 hours or overnight.
- Preheat broiler or grill to medium heat.
- Drain chicken and grill, turning frequently so as not to burn, until cooked through, about 20–30 minutes.
- Brush on the additional mojo and serve.

Serves 4

Zesty Chicken Meatballs

- ½ cup soft bread crumbs
- ¼ cup milk
- 1 egg
- 1 lb ground chicken
- 1 tbs fresh thyme
- ½ cup chopped parsley
- 1 tsp dried oregano
- 1 onion, minced
- 1 clove garlic, minced
- 2 tbs minced chives
- 1 carrot, grated
- ⅓ cup grated Parmesan cheese
- ¼ cup vegetable oil
- 4 cups Italian tomato sauce (page 137)

● Soak the bread crumbs in the milk, add the egg, and combine with all the other ingredients except the oil and tomato sauce. Form into balls.
● Heat the oil in a frying pan and shallow fry the meatballs until light golden.
● Heat the tomato sauce to simmering.
● Place the meatballs in the sauce and simmer for about 30 minutes.
● Serve the meatballs with the tomato sauce and spaghetti.

Makes about 15

Nutmeg-scented Crêpes filled with Chicken & Fresh Herbs

Traditionally these are made with ground beef; here I've lightened the recipe by using ground chicken.

- 1 lb ground chicken
- 1 tsp minced garlic
- 2 tbs olive oil
- ½ cup chopped fresh herbs (chives, parsley, basil, thyme)
- 2 eggs
- ½ cup bread crumbs
- ½ tsp grated nutmeg
- ⅓ cup grated Parmesan cheese
- 3 cups Italian tomato sauce (see opposite)
- 1 cup grated mozzarella cheese

FOR THE CRÊPES
- ¾ cup flour
- pinch of grated nutmeg
- pinch of salt
- 1 cup milk
- 2 eggs
- 1½ tbs melted butter plus more for frying

- To make the crêpes: place the flour, nutmeg and salt in a mixing bowl. Combine the milk with the lightly beaten eggs.
- Make a well in the center of the flour and pour in all the liquid. Gradually beat the flour into the liquid until smooth. Beat in the melted butter. Leave to rest for about 1 hour.
- Heat a 6 inch frying pan, lightly brush with melted butter and pour in about ¼ cup batter. Cook for a few seconds, then flip and cook for a few more seconds. Remove to a plate and repeat with the remaining batter. This quantity of batter should make about 8 crêpes.

- To make the filling: combine the chicken with the garlic. Heat the oil in a sauté pan and add the chicken. Cook until just beginning to brown. Add the herbs and cook for a few minutes longer.
- Put the chicken mixture in a food processor and process until finely chopped.
- Place in a bowl, add the eggs, bread crumbs and nutmeg, and stir to combine. Add the Parmesan cheese. Season with salt and freshly ground black pepper.
- Preheat oven to 375°F.
- To assemble: Place a thin layer of tomato sauce into an ovenproof dish.
- Place a crêpe onto a plate, spoon about 2 tablespoons of filling into the middle, and roll from both ends. Gently place into the prepared dish and repeat with the remaining crêpes.
- Spoon tomato sauce over the crêpes, sprinkle with the mozzarella cheese and bake for 30 minutes until hot and bubbly.

Serves 4–6

Italian Tomato Sauce

- **1 tbs olive oil**
- **1 tsp minced garlic**
- **1 onion, finely chopped**
- **½ cup grated carrots**
- **28 oz can tomatoes, crushed with juice**
- **½ tsp sugar**
- **1 tsp dried Italian herbs (oregano or basil)**

- Heat the olive oil in a saucepan and add the garlic and onion. Sauté until fragrant. Add the carrots, tomatoes, sugar, and salt and freshly ground black pepper. Add the herbs, cover, and simmer for about 30 minutes until the sauce is thick and flavorful.

Makes about 3 cups

Steak & Pineapple Kebabs with Teriyaki Syrup

- **1 lb boneless steak, cut into 1½ inch cubes**
- **1 onion, cut into quarters**
- **1 green bell pepper, cut into pieces**
- **12 pieces fresh pineapple**
- **2 tbs minced chives**
- **2 garlic cloves, minced**
- **2 tbs red wine vinegar**
- **1 tbs vegetable oil**
- **salt and freshly ground black pepper**

FOR THE SYRUP
- **½ cup soy sauce**
- **½ cup rice wine**
- **⅓ cup brown sugar**
- **1 garlic clove, minced**
- **1 tbs minced ginger**

- If using wooden skewers, soak in water overnight.
- Combine the steak pieces with all the remaining ingredients (except those for the syrup) and marinate for 30 minutes.
- To make the syrup: combine all the ingredients in a saucepan and simmer until thick, about 20 minutes.
- Thread the steak, vegetables and fruit onto skewers.
- Grill or barbecue on high heat for about 10 minutes, until the meat is cooked. Brush with the teriyaki syrup, then remove from the heat.

Serves 4–6

Marinated Grilled Lamb in Sesame, Hoisin & Garlic

- **2 tbs hoisin sauce**
- **1 tbs Chinese chili sauce**
- **1 tsp rum**
- **2 tbs tomato ketchup**
- **2 tbs brown sugar**
- **1 tsp sesame oil**
- **2 tbs soy sauce**
- **4 garlic cloves, minced**
- **1 tbs minced ginger**
- **1 tsp freshly ground black pepper**
- **1 lb lamb shoulder chops, loin chops or boneless lamb, about 1–1½ inches thick**

• Combine all the ingredients except the lamb in a mixing bowl. Rub onto the lamb pieces. Cover and marinate for 4 hours.
• Preheat broiler or grill.
• Cook the lamb for about 6 minutes per side. Baste with zesty barbecue sauce and serve.

Serves 4–6

Zesty Barbecue Sauce

- **1 tbs vegetable oil**
- **1 onion, grated or minced**
- **3 garlic cloves, minced**
- **1 cup tomato ketchup**
- **¼ cup brown sugar**
- **1 tbs yellow mustard**
- **2 tbs Worcestershire sauce**
- **1 tsp rum**
- **1 tsp hot pepper sauce**

• Heat the oil in a small saucepan, add the onion and garlic and sauté until fragrant. Add all the other ingredients and cook until the mixture begins to boil. Remove from heat and leave to cool.

Stir-fried Beef with Vegetables on Noodle Cake

- ½ lb egg noodles
- 12 oz beef (sirloin),
  cut into ¼ inch thin slices
- 4 tbs vegetable oil
- 3 tbs minced chives
- 1 tbs minced ginger
- 1 tbs minced garlic
- ⅔ lb mixed vegetables,
  cut into 1½ inch pieces

FOR THE MARINADE
- 2 tbs soy sauce
- 1 tbs rum (optional)
- 2 tsp minced garlic
- 1 tsp sesame oil
- 1 tsp cornstarch

FOR THE SAUCE
- 1 cup chicken stock
- ¼ cup oyster sauce
- 1 tbs soy sauce
- 2 tsp sugar
- 1 tsp sesame oil
- 1 tbs cornstarch
- 5 tbs vegetable oil

- Cook the noodles until tender, according to the manufacturer's directions. Drain and set aside.
- Combine all the marinade ingredients and add the beef. Marinate for about 1 hour or overnight.
- Combine the sauce ingredients and set aside.
- Heat a wok and add 2 tablespoons of oil. Add the beef and stir-fry until it loses its pinkness. Remove.
- Clean the pan, heat 1 tablespoon of oil and add the chives, ginger and garlic. Stir-fry until fragrant.
- Add the vegetables and cover to steam for a few minutes. Add the sauce and stir well until thick. Add the beef slices, toss to coat, then remove from the heat.
- Heat a large frying pan and add the remaining oil. When hot, add the noodles and press into the pan to form a solid mass. Flip the noodle cake and brown the other side.
- Remove from heat to a serving platter, spoon the beef and vegetables over the cake, and serve.

Serves 4

Roast Turkey West Indian Style

This is very much a tradition on all the islands. The stuffing recipe that follows is also a traditional one.

- **12–14 lb turkey**
- **¼ cup fresh thyme**
- **½ cup chopped chives**
- **¼ cup parsley**
- **⅛ cup garlic**
- **¼ cup olive oil**
- **10 cups stuffing**
- **½ cup butter, softened**

• The night before cooking your turkey, rinse the turkey, pat it dry and season it inside and out with salt and freshly ground black pepper.
• Purée the fresh herbs and garlic with the olive oil and rub the mixture over the turkey. Cover and leave refrigerated overnight.

• The next day, bring your turkey to room temperature.
• Preheat oven to 425°F.
• Pack the neck cavity loosely with some of the stuffing, fold the neck skin under the body of the turkey and fasten it with a skewer.
• Pack the body cavity loosely with the remaining stuffing and truss the turkey.
• Rub the turkey with the butter, place it in a roasting pan and roast it in the oven for 30 minutes.
• Reduce the temperature to 325°F.
• Baste the turkey with the pan juices and add 1 cup water to the pan.
• Roast the turkey, basting it every 20 minutes for another 2½–3 hours, or until a meat thermometer inserted into the fleshiest part of the thigh registers 180°F and the juices run clear when the thigh is pierced.
• Transfer the turkey to a platter, remove the string and cover loosely with foil.
• Remove stuffing and leave the turkey to settle before carving.

Serves 10–12

TURKEY COOKING TIMES

Here are some guidelines for you to follow when roasting your turkey. Some recipes will tell you to start the roasting process at a temperature of about 425°F, this is to brown the turkey before the cooking process begins. After about 30 minutes you lower the temperature to 325°F and continue cooking.

WEIGHT	UNSTUFFED	STUFFED
10–18 lb	3–3½ hours	3¾–4½ hours
18–22 lb	3½–4 hours	4–5 hours
22–24 lb	4–4½ hours	4½–5 hours
24–29 lb	4½–5 hours	5½–6¼ hours

Trini Christmas Giblet Stuffing

- 1 lb chicken or turkey giblets
- 1 tbs minced chives plus ½ cup chopped fresh chives
- 1 tsp minced garlic plus
  1 tbs finely chopped garlic
- 4 tbs vegetable oil
- 1 cup finely chopped onions
- 4 tbs fresh French thyme
- 4 pimento peppers,
  seeded and chopped
- 1 hot pepper, seeded and chopped
- ¼ cup chopped celery
- ½ cup currants
- 4 cups soft bread crumbs
- 2 eggs, lightly beaten
- ½ cup toasted pecans,
  chopped (optional)
- 4 oz butter, melted (optional)

• Clean the giblets and mince in a food processor. Season with the minced chives and garlic.

• Heat the oil in a large sauté pan and add the chopped garlic, onions, thyme, peppers, chopped chives and celery and cook and stir until the onions are tender. Add the giblets and stir until they have lost their pinkness, about 2 minutes. Add the currants and season with salt and freshly ground black pepper.

• Add the bread crumbs, eggs and pecans, if using, and combine well. Add the melted butter, if desired, and stir.

• If your stuffing seems too dry, moisten with a little chicken stock, adding only about 1 tablespoon at a time until moist but not wet.

• Turn onto a plate and cool before stuffing into bird.

Serves 8

Braised Lamb with Eggplant & Grilled Polenta

- **6 lamb shoulder slices, cut about 1 inch thick**
- **2 tbs olive oil**
- **2 onions, thinly sliced**
- **8 garlic cloves, finely chopped**
- **1 small eggplant, cubed**
- **14 oz can whole tomatoes, crushed with juice**

FOR THE MARINADE
- **1 tbs minced chives**
- **1 tbs fresh thyme**
- **2 garlic cloves, minced**
- **1 tsp freshly ground black pepper**

- Cut the lamb into 2 inch pieces.
- Combine the ingredients for the marinade.
- Marinate the lamb pieces for 2 hours or overnight.
- Heat the olive oil in a large frying pan and fry the lamb pieces on both sides until the meat is nicely browned. Remove and drain off any extra fat.
- Add a little oil to the pan and sauté the onions and garlic until fragrant, about 4 minutes. Add the eggplant and cook for a few minutes more.
- Return the lamb pieces to the pan. Add the tomatoes. Cover and simmer for about 1 hour, until the lamb is tender, adding a little water at a time to prevent sticking.
- Taste and season with salt and freshly ground black pepper.

Serves 6

Grilled Polenta

- **6 cups water or seasoned broth**
- **2 garlic cloves, chopped**
- **1 tsp salt**
- **1¼ cups yellow cornmeal**
- **¼ cup chopped basil or parsley or other fresh herbs**
- **¼ cup olive oil**

- Bring the water or broth to a boil and add the garlic, salt and some freshly ground black pepper.
- Whisk in the cornmeal in a thin stream and cook over a medium heat for about 35 minutes or until the polenta starts to come away from the pan. Stir in the fresh herbs.
- Pour the polenta onto a lightly greased, shallow serving dish or pie plate and cool.
- Preheat broiler or grill.
- Cut the cooled polenta into squares. Generously brush with olive oil and grill until lightly browned on both sides.

Serves 4–6

144

Stewed Chicken
Trini Style with Ginger

- **4 lb chicken, cut into pieces**
- **1 tbs minced chives**
- **1 tbs French thyme**
- **4 garlic cloves, minced**
- **1 tbs minced ginger**
- **2 pimento peppers, seeded and chopped**
- **1 large onion, thinly sliced**
- **¼ tsp allspice powder**
- **1 tsp salt and freshly ground black pepper**
- **2 tbs vegetable oil**
- **2 tbs brown sugar**

- Rub the chicken with the chives, thyme, garlic, ginger, peppers, onion, allspice, salt and pepper.
- Let marinate for about 1 hour.
- Heat the oil in a large pot. When hot, add the sugar and cook until the sugar becomes very frothy and a very dark brown. When it starts to smoke, add the chicken pieces, and working very quickly, turn the chicken around in the pot to coat evenly with the caramelized sugar and brown.
- Add the marinade ingredients left in the bowl. Turn, and cover the pot. The chicken will start to release its own juices during cooking.
- Lower the heat and continue cooking until the chicken is tender and a rich gravy has formed, about 30 minutes.

Serves 4–6

Stewed Oxtail with Cinnamon Dumplings

- **2 lb oxtail, sliced into ¾ inch pieces**
- **1 tbs minced garlic**
- **1 tbs minced chives**
- **1 tbs red wine vinegar**
- **1 tbs chopped celery**
- **2 tbs vegetable oil**
- **2 tbs brown sugar**
- **1 large sprig of French thyme**
- **1 pimento pepper, seeded and chopped**
- **¼ tsp allspice powder**
- **1 large onion, chopped**
- **1 carrot, chopped**
- **4 cloves**
- **cinnamon dumplings (page 57)**

• Trim the meat of fat, and season with the garlic, chives, vinegar and celery. Set aside for 1 hour.

• Heat the oil in a sauté pan, add the sugar and caramelize to a dark brown color. Add the oxtail slices and turn quickly, browning well on all sides.

• Add the rest of the ingredients, turn well and season with salt and freshly ground black pepper.

• Cook for a few minutes, then turn heat to low and cover. Let cook until tender, about 40 minutes, basting occasionally and adding water only if needed to prevent sticking.

• Meanwhile, divide the dumpling dough into 2 pieces. Form each piece into a long rope-like shape about 12 inches in length. Cut into 3 inch lengths, flatten slightly and drop into boiling water. Cook until the dumplings float to the top of the pot.

• Add the cooked dumplings to the oxtail stew and let simmer for about 15 minutes.

Serves 4–6

MEATS

Chicken & Veggie Shepherd's Pie

A light alternative to the traditional ground beef and mashed potato pie. You could also use ground beef here, or even turkey.

- 1 lb boneless chicken breast, cut into 1 inch cubes
- 1 tbs fresh herb seasoning (page 117)
- ½ tbs chopped celery
- 1 tsp minced garlic
- 2 tbs olive oil
- 1 large onion, chopped
- 2 pimento peppers, seeded and chopped
- ½ hot pepper, seeded and chopped
- 2 tbs flour
- 1 tsp paprika plus extra for sprinkling
- 2 cups milk
- 4 cups cut fresh vegetables (any mixture: cauliflower, carrots, green beans, etc.)

FOR THE TOPPING
- 2 lb potatoes, boiled and crushed
- ½ cup milk
- 3 eggs, beaten
- 1 cup grated cheese (optional)
- ¼ cup chopped chives
- 1 tsp minced garlic

- Marinate the chicken in the herb seasoning, celery, garlic, and salt and freshly ground black pepper for 30 minutes.
- Heat the oil in a sauté pan and add the onion, pimentos and hot pepper. Cook for 4 minutes.
- Add the chicken and cook until no longer pink in color.
- Sprinkle on the flour and combine well. Stir for a few seconds, then add the paprika and milk. Cook until thick and smooth, add the vegetables and cook for 3–4 minutes more.
- Taste and adjust seasoning. When the mixture is thick, remove from heat and turn into a greased casserole dish.
- Preheat oven to 350ºF.
- To make the topping: combine the mashed potatoes with the milk, beaten eggs and cheese, if using, and season with salt and pepper. Add the chives and garlic.
- Top the chicken mixture with the potatoes and sprinkle with additional paprika.
- Bake for 30 minutes until heated through.

Serves 6

Stewed Lamb Neck Slices

- **2 lb lamb neck,
  sliced into ¾ inch pieces**
- **1 tbs minced garlic**
- **1 tbs minced chives**
- **1 tbs red wine vinegar**
- **1 tbs chopped celery**
- **2 tbs vegetable oil**
- **2 tbs brown sugar**
- **1 large sprig of French thyme**
- **1 pimento pepper,
  seeded and chopped**
- **1 large onion, chopped**
- **1 carrot, chopped**
- **4 cloves**

- Trim the meat of fat and season with the garlic, chives, vinegar and celery. Set aside for 1 hour.
- Heat the oil in a sauté pan, add the sugar and caramelize to a dark brown color. Add the pieces of lamb and turn quickly, browning well.
- Add the rest of the ingredients, turn, and season with salt and freshly ground black pepper.
- Cook for a few minutes, then turn heat to low and cover. Let cook until tender, about 40 minutes, basting occasionally and adding water only if needed to prevent sticking.

Serves 4–6

Roasted Chicken with Herb & Currant Stuffing

- **4 lb chicken, washed and cleaned**
- **1 tbs minced garlic**
- **1 tbs fresh herb seasoning (page 117)**
- **1 tbs fresh lime juice**
- **2 tbs olive oil**

FOR THE STUFFING
- **2 tbs olive oil**
- **2 garlic cloves, chopped**
- **1 onion, finely chopped**
- **2 pimento peppers, seeded and chopped**
- **½ hot pepper, seeded and chopped**
- **½ cup chopped fresh herbs**
- **⅓ cup currants or raisins**
- **¾ cup soft bread crumbs**
- **chicken or vegetable stock**

- Remove the backbone from the chicken. Combine all the other ingredients (except for those needed for the stuffing) and spread over the chicken. Let marinate for 30–40 minutes.
- To make the stuffing: heat the oil in a sauté pan, add the garlic, onion and peppers and sauté until tender and fragrant, about 5 minutes.
- Add the herbs and currants, stir to combine, then add ½ cup bread crumbs and stir. Add the remaining crumbs gradually, adding a little stock to moisten – don't make your mixture too dry or wet, it should just hold together. Season with salt and freshly ground black pepper. Place stuffing on a plate to cool.
- Preheat oven to 375ºF.
- Take chicken and loosen the skin. Push the stuffing under the chicken skin.
- Place on a baking tray and bake for 30–40 minutes until the juices run clear.

Serves 4

Chicken Cooked with Indian Spices

A great change from the traditional curry,
this dish sings with exotic spices. Serve with roti or rice.

- **1½ lb boneless chicken**
- **1 tbs ground cardamom**
- **½ tbs black pepper**
- **½ tsp salt**
- **2 tbs vegetable oil**
- **1 large onion, sliced**
- **1 cinnamon stick**
- **6 cloves**
- **1 hot pepper, seeded and chopped**
- **1 tbs minced garlic**
- **1 tbs grated ginger**
- **½ tbs ground coriander**
- **½ tbs ground cumin (geera)**
- **½ tbs chili powder**
- **½ tsp turmeric powder**
- **1 cup evaporated milk**
- **1 cup chicken stock**
- **juice of 1 lime**
- **1 tsp garam masala**
- **2 tbs chopped cilantro (chadon beni)**

- On a plate, combine the chicken with the cardamom, black pepper and salt.
- Heat 1 tablespoon of the oil in a sauté pan and brown the chicken pieces. Remove and set aside.
- Add the rest of the oil to the pan. Add the onion, cinnamon, cloves, pepper, garlic and ginger and stir-fry until the mixture becomes a light brown color, adding a little water if necessary to prevent sticking. Cook in this way for about 3–4 minutes.
- In a small bowl combine the coriander, cumin, chili powder and turmeric.
- Now add this mixture to the pan and stir-fry for a few minutes more.
- Return the chicken to the pan and stir well to coat with the spice mixture.
- Add the evaporated milk and stir to combine. Simmer chicken for about 20–30 minutes until tender, adding a little stock from time to time to prevent sticking. When all the stock has been added the chicken should be thick and creamy; if not, cook for a little longer.
- Sprinkle on the lime juice, garam masala and cilantro.

Serves 4–6

Note
Garam masala is an east Indian blend of dried spices consisting of coriander seed, cardamom seed, black geera seed, cloves, black peppercorns, nutmeg and mace. The proportions of the above will vary according to the cook's specific recipe. Garam masala may also be purchased in Indian markets and in some supermarkets.

MEATS

151

Mexican Tamale Pie

*A delicious twist on the traditional tamales,
you can substitute black beans and chicken for the ground beef
and red beans.
This pie is a favorite with kids!*

- **2 lb lean ground beef**
- **2 tbs fresh herb seasoning (page 117)**
- **2 tbs vegetable oil**
- **2 large onions, chopped**
- **6 garlic cloves**
- **3 tbs chili powder**
- **1 tsp ground cumin (geera)**
- **¼ tsp allspice powder**
- **28 oz can whole tomatoes, finely chopped**
- **15 oz can black or red beans**
- **1 cup chopped green olives**
- **⅓ cup chopped cilantro (chadon beni)**

FOR THE TOPPING
- **1 cup all-purpose flour**
- **1 cup cornmeal**
- **1½ tbs sugar**
- **2 tsp baking powder**
- **1 tsp ground cumin (geera)**
- **½ tsp salt**
- **1 egg**
- **1⅓ cups milk**
- **4 tbs melted butter**
- **4 oz grated cheese**
- **¼ cup chopped cilantro (chadon beni)**

- Preheat oven to 375°F.
- Season the meat with the herb seasoning.
- Heat the oil in a sauté pan and add the onion and garlic. Add the beef and brown thoroughly. Add the chili, cumin and allspice, and season with salt and freshly ground black pepper.
- Add the tomatoes, beans and olives, combine, and cover. Simmer for about 20 minutes. Add the cilantro and remove from the heat.
- To make the topping: combine all the dry ingredients in a large mixing bowl. Beat the egg with the milk and add the melted butter. Add to the dry ingredients. Stir in the cheese and cilantro.
- Stir well. The batter may be a little soft but will soon firm up, as the cornmeal tends to absorb a lot of liquid. If the batter seems too dry, add a little milk. The consistency should be like muffin batter.
- Grease a medium-sized casserole dish and spread some batter onto the bottom. Spoon the beef mixture onto this, then top with the remaining corn batter.
- Bake for 30 minutes until risen and golden.

Serves 4

Stuffed Chicken Breasts with Bulghur & Shiitake Mushrooms

- **1 cup bulghur wheat, soaked in warm water for 30 minutes**
- **4 dried black mushrooms, soaked in warm water for 2 hours**
- **4 garlic cloves**
- **½ tsp freshly ground black pepper**
- **1 tsp sesame oil**
- **1½ lb boneless chicken breasts (about 6 chicken breasts)**
- **2 tbs vegetable oil**
- **1 large onion, finely chopped**
- **½ cup chopped chives**
- **2 pimento peppers, seeded and chopped**
- **2 tbs fresh thyme**
- **2 tbs raisins**
- **½ cup chicken stock**
- **¼ cup pine nuts, toasted**
- **¼ cup chopped parsley**

• Strain bulghur and squeeze out any extra liquid. Remove stems from mushrooms, discard, and chop the mushrooms.
• Mince 2 garlic cloves and combine with the black pepper and sesame oil.
• Prepare the chicken breasts by placing each breast between 2 sheets of waxed paper; pound the breasts until about ¼ inch thick. Season with the garlic and black pepper mixture.

• Prepare the stuffing: heat half the vegetable oil in a large sauté pan, add the remaining garlic, chopped, and the onion, and sauté until fragrant. Add the chives, pimento peppers and thyme. Stir and fry for 4 minutes until all the herbs become fragrant.
• Add the mushrooms together with the bulghur and raisins. Stir to combine, gradually adding the chicken stock. Stir until stuffing comes together. Add the pine nuts and parsley.
• Taste and adjust seasoning. Leave stuffing to cool.
• Preheat oven to 350ºF.
• Place about 1 tablespoon of stuffing on each chicken breast, roll each breast up and hold together with small metal skewers.
• Heat the remaining oil in a sauté pan and sauté the chicken breasts until brown. Remove to a heatproof baking dish and bake for 30 minutes.
• Remove chicken breasts from dish and take out skewers. Leave breasts to settle, then slice and serve. (You could make a sauce using the drippings from the baking dish.)

Serves 6

Spinach-stuffed Chicken Breasts

- **4 boneless chicken breasts**
- **1 tsp minced garlic plus 1 garlic clove, chopped**
- **1 tsp minced chives**
- **½ lb cleaned spinach**
- **1 tbs vegetable oil**
- **1 small onion, finely chopped**
- **½ hot pepper, seeded and chopped**
- **4 oz feta cheese**
- **¼ tsp grated nutmeg**
- **2 tsp olive oil**

- Preheat oven to 350ºF.
- Flatten the chicken breasts between 2 pieces of waxed paper. Marinate in the minced garlic and chives.
- Chop the spinach.
- Heat the vegetable oil in a sauté pan and sauté the onion, pepper and garlic until fragrant. Add the spinach and cook until wilted. Season with salt and freshly ground black pepper, remove and leave to cool.
- Crumble the feta cheese over the spinach and combine. Add the nutmeg.
- Place 1 tablespoon of filling onto the center of the lower half of each chicken breast and fold over to cover. Secure with wooden toothpicks.
- Heat the olive oil in a frying pan and add the stuffed chicken to the pan. Cook just to brown or sear each side.
- Remove to an ovenproof dish and continue cooking in the oven for 20 minutes, until tender.
- Slice and serve.

Serves 4

rice & provisions

Ground provisions are a staple in Caribbean diets and were brought to the Caribbean by our African ancestors, while the delightful breadfruit was brought by Captain Bligh in 1793, as food for the slaves on the sugar plantations. Provisions (yams, sweet potatoes, taro root, cassava, eddoes, tannia) are available year round and provide a great source of carbohydrates at very economical prices. Rice is another staple and is often served with stewed peas, the most popular being red beans, black-eyed peas, pigeon peas and lentil peas. This section showcases provisions and rice in stylish ways that still retain a Caribbean identity. The earthy flavors of provisions make them perfect vehicles for a myriad of other flavors. Recipes like sweet potato salad dressed with herbed vinaigrette can accompany any type of grilled meat, and crushed cassava with lemon and parsley will liven up any meal.

The rice recipes often add the traditional peas or other vegetables, as in black-eyed peas and rice cookup and peppery pumpkin rice. Sometimes the rice is cooked in coconut milk or stock, infused with fresh herbs and fired up with hot peppers – the perfect accompaniment to any meal!

Hot & Spicy Jump-up Pigeon Pea Pilaf

Pigeon peas are plentiful in the Caribbean from December to March; we love to use them any which way we can as they are tender, sweet and wholesome.

- **1 tbs vegetable oil**
- **1 onion, finely chopped**
- **1 garlic clove, chopped**
- **1 Congo pepper,
  seeded and chopped, or to taste**
- **1 pimento pepper,
  seeded and chopped**
- **1 cup pigeon peas (gungo peas)**
- **1 cup parboiled rice**
- **1 cup coconut milk**
- **1½ cups broth or water**
- **1 tbs cilantro (chadon beni)**

- Preheat a sauté pan or saucepan, add the oil and heat. Add the onion, garlic and peppers and sauté until fragrant. Season with salt and freshly ground black pepper.
- Add the pigeon peas and stir. Add the rice and toss to combine. Add the coconut milk and broth or water. Stir to combine.
- Bring to a boil, cover and simmer for 20 minutes until the rice is tender. Taste and adjust seasoning.
- Fluff with a fork and sprinkle with cilantro before serving.

Serves 4–6

For a lighter dish
Omit the coconut milk and add half a cup more broth.

West Indian Spinach Rice with Nutmeg & Peppers

West Indian spinach must be cooked before eating as it tends to be very bitter if eaten raw.
Here it makes a wonderful and nutritious rice that even children will love!

- 2 tbs vegetable oil
- 1 large onion, minced
- 2 garlic cloves, minced
- 1 pimento pepper, seeded and chopped
- ½ hot pepper, seeded and chopped
- 4 cups fresh spinach leaves, cleaned, washed and chopped
- 1 tsp salt
- 1 tsp freshly ground black pepper
- ½ tsp grated nutmeg
- 1 cup parboiled rice
- 2½ cups vegetable or chicken stock
- 1 tbs butter

- Heat the oil in a medium-sized saucepan and add the onion, garlic and pimento. Cook for a few minutes, taking care not to burn them.
- Add the hot pepper and stir, then add the spinach and combine. Lower the heat and cover. Cook until the spinach is tender.
- Season with the salt, pepper and grated nutmeg.
- Add the rice and stir to combine. Pour in the stock and cook to boiling. When holes appear at the top of the rice, cover and simmer for 20 minutes. Add butter and gently stir.

Serves 4

Spinach Coconut Rice

- Substitute 1 cup coconut milk for 1 cup stock.

Sweet Potato Gnocchi with Callaloo

This is a Caribbean twist on the traditional Italian gnocchi. The combination of the sweet potatoes and callaloo (taro leaves) makes a rich and wholesome dish.

- 1 tbs vegetable oil
- 4 large callaloo (taro) leaves, washed and chopped
- 1 sweet potato (about 12 oz)
- 4 oz cheese, grated
- 2 tbs butter
- 1 egg yolk
- ¼ tsp grated nutmeg
- ¼–½ cup flour
- 1 cup milk

- Heat the oil and add the callaloo. Cook until soft, about 10 minutes, adding a little stock or water to prevent sticking. Remove and leave to cool.
- Boil the sweet potato, peel and mash with 2 oz cheese, the butter and egg yolk. Season with salt and freshly ground black pepper. Add the nutmeg.
- Add half the cooked callaloo and combine. Add the flour, 1 tablespoon at a time, just enough to make a soft dough.
- Bring a large pot of water to a rolling boil. Add salt.
- Divide the sweet potato mixture into 4 pieces. Roll each piece into a log about 1 inch thick and cut into ¾ inch pieces. Drop the pieces into the boiling water, cook until they float to the top, remove and drain. Place in a large bowl.
- Pour the milk into a saucepan, bring to a boil, add salt, pepper and some more nutmeg if desired. Stir in the rest of the callaloo and cheese and cook until thick.
- Spoon over the gnocchi and serve.

Serves 4–6

Sweet Potato Mash

- **1 sweet potato (about 12 oz)**
- **2 russet potatoes**
- **½ cup milk**
- **2 tbs vegetable oil**
- **1 onion, chopped**
- **2 garlic cloves, chopped**
- **1 pimento pepper, seeded and chopped**
- **¼ cup chopped chives**
- **½ cup grated cheese (optional)**

- Boil both types of potato, peel and mash.

- Add the milk, salt and freshly ground black pepper and combine.
- Heat the oil in a small frying pan and sauté the onion, garlic and pepper for just 1 minute.
- Add to the potatoes, and add the chives and cheese, if using. Place in an ovenproof dish and sprinkle with cheese if desired.
- Broil or grill until the cheese is melted and the top is browned. Garnish with chopped chives.

Serves 4–6

Breadfruit Sauté

- **2 tbs vegetable oil**
- **2 onions, sliced**
- **2 pimento peppers, seeded and cut into strips**
- **½ Congo pepper, seeded and chopped**
- **1 garlic clove, chopped**
- **1 lb breadfruit, peeled, boiled and cut into 2 inch pieces**
- **¼ cup chopped celery**
- **¼ cup chopped parsley**
- **2 tbs fresh thyme**

- Heat the oil in a large non-stick frying pan and add the onion, peppers and garlic. Sauté until fragrant, then add the breadfruit, turn and toss until the pieces become coated with the onion and garlic mixture.
- Add the celery and fresh herbs and season with salt and freshly ground black pepper. Continue cooking over a medium heat, scraping the bottom of the pan to prevent sticking. Cook for 10 minutes or until the breadfruit pieces are golden in color.
- Taste and adjust seasoning.

Serves 4–6

Sweet Potato Cakes

- 2 lb sweet potatoes
- ½ cup milk
- ¼ cup butter
- ⅓ cup chopped fresh herbs
- ¼ tsp grated nutmeg
- 1 egg
- 1 cup flour
- 1 cup bread crumbs
- vegetable oil for frying

● Boil, peel and mash the sweet potatoes.
● Warm the milk with the butter and add to the potatoes. Mix well, add the herbs and nutmeg, and season to taste with salt.
● Beat the egg and set aside.
● Place the flour on one plate, and the bread crumbs on another.
● Form the potato into 2 inch balls, dredge in flour, shake off the excess, then dip in egg and roll in the crumbs. Flatten and pan fry in oil until golden.

Makes 6–8

Red Bean & Pumpkin Pilaf

- 1 tbs vegetable oil
- 1 garlic clove, minced
- 1 large onion, chopped
- 1 pimento pepper, seeded and chopped
- 1 Congo pepper
- 1 tbs thyme
- 1 cup chopped pumpkin
- 14 oz can red beans, drained
- 1 cup parboiled rice
- 2½ cups chicken stock
- 2 tsp butter

● Heat a heavy saucepan, add the oil and heat. Add the garlic, onion, chopped pimento, whole Congo pepper and thyme, and sauté until fragrant.
● Add the pumpkin and stir. Add the beans, then the rice and toss to combine. Add the stock.
● Bring to a boil, then lower the heat and simmer for 20 minutes until the rice is tender. If it seems too wet, remove lid and let the rice dry out a bit.
● Before serving, remove the hot pepper, add salt and freshly ground black pepper to taste and stir in the butter.

Serves 4–6

Peppery Pumpkin Rice

- **1 tbs vegetable oil**
- **2 garlic cloves**
- **1 onion, thinly sliced**
- **1 hot pepper**
- **2 pimento peppers, seeded and chopped**
- **1 sprig of thyme**
- **1 cup chopped calabaza pumpkin**
- **1 cup rice**
- **2½ cups vegetable or chicken stock**
- **1 tsp salt**
- **1 tbs butter**
- **2 tbs toasted pumpkin seeds**

• Heat the oil in a saucepan and add the garlic, onion, peppers and thyme. Sauté until fragrant. Add the pumpkin and stir. Add the rice and cook for a few seconds more.

• Add the stock and salt. Bring to a boil, lower the heat, cover and cook until tender, about 20 minutes.

• Before serving, remove the hot pepper, add the butter and pumpkin seeds and fluff the rice.

Serves 4

Sweet Potato Hash Browns

This recipe uses leftover sweet potatoes. Simply peel, if necessary, and cut into tiny squares.

• Heat some vegetable oil in a pan and sauté some chopped onion, garlic and pimento peppers.

• Add the sweet potatoes and cook, mashing them a little so that they come together. When they start to brown, add some chopped chives and celery and cook for a few minutes more. Season with salt and freshly ground black pepper.

Baked Sweet Potatoes
with Chili & Lemon

- **2 large sweet potatoes, about 1½–2 lb**
- **¼ cup olive oil**
- **1 tbs minced garlic**
- **1 tsp chili powder**
- **salt and freshly ground black pepper**
- **2 tbs fresh lemon juice**

- Boil the sweet potatoes, peel and cut into wedges.
- Preheat broiler or grill.
- Combine all the other ingredients, brush over the potatoes on both sides and place into a greased ovenproof pan.
- Grill or broil until golden on top. Turn and repeat. Remove and serve at once.

Serves 4–6

Creamed Cassava with Lemon Parsley Gremolata

This recipe can also be made with potatoes
or any type of ground provision.

- **2 lb cassava**
- **½ cup milk**
- **2 tbs butter**

FOR THE GREMOLATA
- **1 tsp lemon zest, finely grated**
- **2 garlic cloves, minced**
- **¼ cup finely chopped parsley**

• Boil the cassava in a large pan of water for about 20–30 minutes, until very soft. Drain and remove the inner core.

• Heat the milk with the butter. Add to the drained cassava and crush the cassava until creamy. Add salt to taste.

• To make the gremolata: mix all the ingredients together.

• Add the gremolata to the crushed cassava and stir.

Serves 4–6

For a lighter dish
Use olive oil in place of butter.

Caribbean Rice Pilaf

- **2 large dried Chinese black mushrooms**
- **1 tbs vegetable oil**
- **1 clove garlic, minced**
- **½ cup chopped red bell pepper**
- **1 onion, finely chopped**
- **1½ cups parboiled rice**
- **½ cup raisins**
- **3 tbs chopped chives**

FOR THE SAUCE
- **2½ cups chicken stock**
- **1 tbs rum (optional)**
- **1 tbs light soy sauce**
- **1 tsp sesame oil**
- **1 tsp Chinese chili sauce**
- **½ tsp salt**
- **1 tsp grated orange peel**

- Soak the black mushrooms in 2 cups warm water for 2 hours.
- Drain the mushrooms, remove the stems, discard, and slice the mushrooms.
- To make the sauce: combine all the ingredients in a small bowl and stir well.
- Heat the oil in a saucepan. Add the garlic, pepper and onion and sauté until fragrant.
- Add the rice and stir to coat. Add the raisins and sauce, cover, and simmer until cooked, about 20 minutes.
- Remove from the heat and stir in the chives.

Serves 4–6

Shredded Plantain Fritters

You can use any type of ground provision in this recipe.

- **1 tsp salt**
- **1 tsp freshly ground black pepper**
- **½ tsp chili powder**
- **2 large green plantains, peeled and grated coarsely**
- **1 large onion, finely sliced**
- **6 garlic cloves, minced**
- **1 cup vegetable oil for frying**

• Combine the salt, pepper and chili powder.
• Combine the plantain, onion and garlic – the mixture will be sticky.
• Heat the oil in a frying pan.
• Using your hands or two spoons, form the plantain mixture into 1 inch balls, taking care not to compact the balls. Carefully drop the plantain balls into the oil and fry until golden, about 2 minutes, turning once.
• Drain and sprinkle with the salt mixture.

Makes 12–15

Oven-roasted Sweet Potato Chili Fries

- **1 tbs vegetable oil**
- **2 tsp chili powder**
- **½ tsp salt**
- **½ tsp dried oregano**
- **¼ tsp garlic powder**
- **¼ tsp ground cumin (geera)**
- **1½ lb sweet potatoes, peeled and cut into wedges**

- Preheat oven to 450ºF.
- Combine all the ingredients except the potatoes in a bowl.
- Add the cut potatoes to the bowl and toss to coat evenly.
- Place the potatoes in a single layer on a greased baking sheet and bake for 35 minutes until golden brown.

Serves 4

Aromatic Rice Pilaf

- **1 tsp vegetable oil**
- **1 small onion, chopped**
- **½ tsp saffron powder**
- **½ tsp ground cinnamon**
- **1 cup rice**
- **½ cup fresh or frozen mixed vegetables**
- **2¼ cups chicken stock, skimmed and fat removed**

- Heat the oil in a medium-sized saucepan, add the onion and cook until fragrant. Add the spices and rice and cook for a few seconds longer, then add the vegetables and stock.
- Bring to a boil, lower the heat and cover. Simmer until the rice is tender, about 20 minutes.
- Fluff with a fork before serving.

Serves 4

Spiced Rice with Lentils & Caramelized Onions

Rice and peas dishes are a staple in all Caribbean countries. Here, another popular pea, lentil, is cooked with rice and spiced up with Indian spices.

- 2 tbs vegetable oil
- 4 cups sliced onions
- 3 cloves
- 2 allspice berries
- 1 tsp ground cumin (geera)
- 6 cardamom pods, crushed
- 1 tsp crushed garlic
- 1 cup parboiled rice
- ½ cup dried lentils, cooked until tender and drained
- 2½ cups vegetable or chicken stock
- 1 tsp salt
- 1 cup chopped fresh herbs

- Preheat oven to 350°F.
- Heat 1 tablespoon of the oil in a large frying pan and add the onions. Cook on a medium low heat, stirring, until caramelized or dark brown in color and tender, about 15–20 minutes. Remove from the heat and set aside.
- Heat the remaining oil in a medium-sized saucepan, and add the spices and garlic. Stir and fry for a couple of minutes, then add rice and stir to coat, followed by the lentils. Stir, and add the stock. Bring to a boil, season with salt and add the fresh herbs.
- Cover and steam until the rice is tender, about 20 minutes. Remove the spices and set aside.
- Place the onions in the bottom of an ovenproof skillet or dish with a flat base and high sides. Spoon the rice mixture on top and press down firmly to compact the rice.
- Bake for 20 minutes. Cool a little before unmolding.

Serves 4–6

Taro Root Loaf with Fresh Herbs

- **1 lb ground chicken or beef**
- **dash of aromatic bitters**
- **½ cup chopped fresh herbs (chives, thyme, parsley and celery)**
- **2 tbs vegetable oil**
- **2 garlic cloves, chopped**
- **2 pimento peppers, seeded and chopped**
- **1 onion, chopped**
- **½ cup canned tomatoes with juice**
- **1 lb taro root, peeled and boiled until very tender**
- **2 tbs butter**
- **½–¾ cup milk**
- **1 egg, beaten**
- **4 basil leaves (optional)**
- **½ cup grated cheese**

- Combine the meat with the bitters, herbs, salt and freshly ground black pepper.
- Heat the oil in a sauté pan, add the garlic, peppers and onion and cook until tender and fragrant, about 2–3 minutes.
- Add the meat mixture and turn to brown and cook for a few minutes until the chicken, if using, loses its pinkness.
- Add the tomatoes and bring to a boil. Cover and simmer for 20 minutes until cooked and tender. Taste and adjust seasonings. Remove from the heat.
- Crush the taro root to a creamy consistency. Add the butter, milk and egg and mix well – a hand-held beater works well here. The mixture should be fluffy and creamy. Taste and adjust the seasoning.
- Butter a medium-sized casserole dish. Preheat oven to 400ºF.
- Line the base of the dish with half the taro root and place the meat mixture on top. Top with the basil leaves, if using, then spoon over the remaining taro root. Sprinkle with cheese.
- Bake until lightly browned and heated through, about 20 minutes.

Serves 4–6

Curried Pigeon Pea Pilaf

- **1 tbs vegetable oil**
- **1 onion, finely chopped**
- **1 garlic clove, chopped**
- **1 pimento pepper, seeded and chopped**
- **1 hot pepper, seeded and chopped, or to taste**
- **1 tbs curry powder**
- **1 cup cooked pigeon peas**
- **1 cup parboiled rice**
- **1 cup coconut milk**
- **1½ cups broth or water**
- **¼ cup chopped cilantro (chadon beni) (optional)**

- Preheat a sauté pan or saucepan, add the oil and heat. Add the onion, garlic and peppers and sauté until fragrant.
- Mix the curry powder with ¼ cup water, add to the pot, and stir until the curry comes together and most of the water has evaporated. Season with salt and freshly ground black pepper.
- Add the pigeon peas and stir. Add the rice, toss to combine, then add the coconut milk and broth or water. Stir to combine.
- Bring to a boil, cover and simmer for 20 minutes until the rice is tender. Taste and adjust seasoning.
- Garnish with cilantro, if desired, and fluff with a fork before serving.

Serves 4–6

For a lighter dish
Use all broth in place of the coconut milk or use low fat coconut milk.

Grilled Cassava with Lime Garlic Sauce

- **2 lb cassava, boiled and drained**
- **⅓ cup olive oil or vegetable oil**
- **1 tbs chopped garlic**
- **2 tbs fresh lime juice**
- **2 tbs chopped cilantro (chadon beni)**

- Remove the inner vein from the cassava. Cut the cassava into 2 inch lengths and place in a shallow baking dish.
- Heat the oil in a small saucepan, add the garlic, lime, and salt and freshly ground black pepper. Sauté for a few minutes, without browning the garlic.
- Add the cilantro, stir and pour the mixture over the cassava.
- Preheat broiler or grill.
- Place the cassava under broiler and broil until it is hot and the edges are browned.

Serves 4–6

Creamy Garlicky Yams

You can drizzle the mashed yams with a little truffle oil, which gives a delicious earthy flavor

- **2 lb yams, peeled**
- **1 tsp butter**
- **½ cup milk**
- **1 garlic clove, minced**
- **¼ cup chopped parsley**

• Cut the yams into small pieces and boil in salted water for about 20 minutes or until tender.
• Drain and mash with the butter, milk and garlic. Season to taste with salt and freshly ground black pepper. Sprinkle with parsley.

Serves 4–6

Baked Vegetable Rice Casserole

- **1 cup parboiled rice**
- **2 tbs vegetable oil**
- **1 large onion, finely chopped**
- **1 bell pepper, finely chopped**
- **½ cup Italian tomato sauce (page 137)**
- **14 oz can peas and carrots or 1 cup chopped fresh vegetables, steamed**
- **½ cup milk**
- **1 egg, beaten**
- **1 cup grated Cheddar cheese**

FOR THE GRATIN
- **⅓ cup dry bread crumbs**
- **⅓ cup grated cheese**
- **⅓ cup finely chopped parsley**

- Boil the rice and leave to cool.
- Heat the oil in a sauté pan and add the onion and pepper. Sauté until fragrant. Add the tomato sauce and cook until the mixture is well combined and the onions are tender, about 10 minutes.
- Combine the rice with the tomato mixture and add the vegetables.
- Mix the milk with the egg and Cheddar cheese. Add to the rice mixture.
- Preheat oven to 375ºF.
- Turn the rice mixture into a greased casserole dish.
- To make the gratin: combine all the ingredients. Spoon on top of the rice.
- Bake for 25–30 minutes.

Serves 4

Cinnamon Curried Fried Rice

- 1 cup rice
- 1 large cinnamon stick
- 3 tsp vegetable oil
- 1 egg, beaten
- 6 garlic cloves, minced
- 1 carrot, cut into small cubes
- ½ cup chopped chives
- 1 tbs curry powder
- 1 cup frozen green peas
- 1 tsp sugar
- 3 tbs soy sauce

- Boil the rice with the cinnamon stick and leave to cool.
- Heat a wok, add 1 teaspoon of the oil and fry the beaten egg. Remove and slice egg into strips.
- Clean the wok, heat and add the remaining oil. Add the garlic and stir-fry until fragrant. Add the carrot and stir-fry until tender. Add the chives, combine, then return the egg to the wok.
- Add the curry powder and stir to combine, then add the peas and rice and stir-fry for another minute.
- Add the sugar and soy sauce together with a few tablespoons of water if necessary.
- Stir-fry for a further minute. Remove from heat and serve.

Serves 4–6

Black-eyed Peas & Rice Cookup

- **1 tbs vegetable oil**
- **1 onion, chopped**
- **1 tbs chopped celery**
- **1 tbs chopped thyme**
- **2 garlic cloves, chopped**
- **2 pimento peppers,
  seeded and chopped**
- **2 tomatoes, chopped**
- **1 cup cooked black-eyed peas**
- **1 cup parboiled rice**
- **1 cup vegetable or chicken stock**
- **½ cup coconut milk**
- **1 tsp salt**
- **1 hot pepper**

- Heat the oil in a heavy medium-sized saucepan and add the onion, celery, thyme, garlic and pimento peppers. Sauté until fragrant and the onion is tender, then add the tomatoes and cook for 1 minute longer.
- Add the peas and rice and turn to coat. Add the stock and coconut milk and bring to a boil. Season with salt and freshly ground black pepper, add the hot pepper and turn the heat to low.
- Cover and steam until cooked, about 20 minutes. Remove hot pepper and serve.

Serves 4

For a lighter dish
Replace the coconut milk with more stock or use low fat coconut milk.

Provision Pie

Anywhere that provisions are served in the Caribbean you are sure to find a pie made with crushed provisions, butter and milk, much like a mashed potato pie – always delicious and hard to resist! Any type of provisions works well in this delicious pie. In this lighter recipe butter is not used, as I have sautéed the aromatics in vegetable oil.

- **3 lb assorted provisions**
- **2 tbs vegetable oil**
- **1½ tbs chopped pimento**
- **1 hot pepper, seeded and chopped**
- **1 large onion, thinly sliced**
- **2 tbs flour**
- **2 cups milk**
- **½ tsp salt**
- **⅛ tsp grated nutmeg**
- **3 tbs chopped chives**
- **1 cup grated cheese**

- Preheat oven to 375°F.
- Peel, boil and cube the provisions. Leave to cool.
- Heat the oil in a sauté pan and add the pimento, hot pepper and onion. Cook for a few minutes.
- Add the flour and stir well. Add the milk and stir. Cook until the sauce is smooth and thick. Season with the salt, some freshly ground black pepper and the nutmeg. Add the provisions and chives. Place in a greased baking dish and sprinkle with the cheese.
- Bake for 10–15 minutes until bubbling and the cheese is melted.

Serves 4–6

PROVISIONS WITH PEPPERS AND HERBS

vegetables & sides

Caribbean people love to eat vegetables cooked as a side dish to their entrée. This section showcases some of our more popular vegetables. Calabaza or West Indian pumpkin, rich, dense and bright orange in color, is a favorite vegetable and is sensational when made into a gratin. Spinach is cooked in coconut milk, giving it a delightful flavor and creamy texture, while eggplant is made into a cake, baked and spiced up with a flavorful tomato sauce, and bitter melons are stuffed with seafood for an exotic twist to a traditional Indian dish. There are also plantains baked with orange juice and rum, and ochroes cooked with corn for a delightful Creole flavor. Of course all these vegetables are infused with local spices and herbs for that perfect Caribbean home flavor!

The above are just a few of the exciting vegetable recipes that await you on the following pages.

Sweet Potato Galettes

- **2 lb sweet potatoes**
- **¼ cup unsalted butter, melted**
- **¼ cup olive oil**
- **2 tbs chopped chives**
- **2 tbs chopped cilantro (chadon beni)**

• Boil the sweet potatoes in their skins until just cooked – they need to be a little undercooked. Peel and refrigerate overnight.

• Grate the potatoes on the coarsest edge of a hand grater.

• Mix the butter and oil and add a little to a frying pan. When hot, add about ½ cup grated potato. Spread it out in the pan and sauté over moderate heat for about 4–5 minutes, until the bottom has crusted and browned. Keep pressing the potato together. Season with salt and freshly ground black pepper.

• Turn and continue cooking until brown.

• Remove from pan and continue with the rest of the grated potato.

• Sprinkle with the chives and cilantro before serving.

Makes about 8

Sautéed Spinach with Nutmeg

- **1 large bunch of spinach, picked over and washed**
- **2 tbs olive oil**
- **1 large onion, chopped**
- **2 garlic cloves, chopped**
- **½ hot pepper, seeded and chopped**
- **¼ tsp grated nutmeg**

- Chop the spinach.
- Heat the oil in a sauté pan and add the onion, garlic and pepper. Sauté until fragrant.
- Add the spinach and cook until wilted. Add the nutmeg and salt and freshly ground black pepper.
- Cover and steam cook for about 15 minutes, adding as little water as possible.
- Adjust seasoning and serve.

Serves 4

Vegetable Stew with Chickpeas

- 1 large eggplant
- 2 tbs olive oil
- 6 garlic cloves, peeled and chopped
- 3 medium onions, chopped coarsely
- 1 large bell pepper, seeded and chopped into large pieces
- 4 ripe tomatoes, cut into quarters
- 1 tsp dried oregano
- 1 tbs fresh thyme
- 1 bay leaf
- 1½ cups cooked chickpeas
- 3 tbs chopped fresh basil or parsley

- Cut the eggplant into 1 inch cubes, sprinkle with salt, and wait for 15 minutes. Rinse.
- Heat the olive oil in a sauté pan and sauté the garlic and onions until fragrant. Add the eggplant and cook for a few minutes. Add the pepper and tomatoes, followed by the oregano, thyme and bay leaf, cooking between additions.
- Add the chickpeas, stir, and season with salt and freshly ground black pepper. Continue to cook over a low heat until the vegetables are submerged in their own liquid.
- Increase the heat and bring the juices to a boil. Immediately lower the heat and simmer, partially covered, for about 1 hour.
- Add the basil or parsley and stir.
- Drain the vegetables and reduce the juices over a high flame until syrupy. Pour over vegetables and adjust seasoning.

Serves 6–8

Sautéed Carailli

- **1 lb carailli (bitter melon), seeds removed, cut into ½ inch pieces**
- **2 tbs vegetable oil**
- **4 onions, sliced**
- **1 pimento pepper, seeded and chopped**
- **6 garlic cloves, chopped**
- **1 tomato, chopped**
- **½ hot pepper, seeded and chopped (optional)**

- If desired, salt the carailli. Let stand for about 20 minutes, then squeeze and rinse under cool water.
- Heat the oil in a sauté pan. Add the onions, pepper and garlic and sauté until fragrant. Add the carailli, tomato, and hot pepper, if using.
- Cover and cook, adding only enough water to prevent sticking. Cook until tender, about 15 minutes.

Serves 4

Stuffed Carailli

- 4 large caraillis (bitter melons)
- 4 garlic cloves
- 2 onions
- 1 hot pepper, seeded
- 2 tbs chopped cilantro (chadon beni)
- 4 tbs vegetable oil
- 1 tsp ground roasted cumin (geera)
- 1 lb shrimp, minced
- 2 stalks lemongrass, chopped
- 1 tsp garam masala (see page 151)
- 3 tbs curry powder
- 1 cup coconut milk

• Slit the caraillis lengthways but do not cut in half or let the knife go right through. Remove the seeds.

• Place the garlic, onion, pepper and cilantro in a blender or food processor and process to a fine consistency.

• Bring a pot of water to a boil, drop in the caraillis and cook for 5 minutes. Remove and drain.

• Heat 1 tablespoon of the oil in a sauté pan and add 1 tablespoon of the ground garlic and onion mixture, together with the cumin. Cook until fragrant. Add the shrimp and cook for 5 minutes. Remove and season to taste with salt.

• Stuff the caraillis with the shrimp mixture, tie together with kitchen string and secure well. Set aside.

• Heat the remaining oil in a sauté pan. Add the lemongrass and the rest of the garlic and onion mixture. Add the garam masala and curry powder. Pour in the coconut milk and simmer for 5 minutes, then add the caraillis and cover and simmer for 10 minutes.

• Slice and serve as a side dish with other curried dishes.

Serves 6–8

Curried Potatoes & Vegetables

- **2 tbs vegetable oil**
- **1 onion, chopped**
- **2 garlic cloves, chopped**
- **1 tbs chopped ginger**
- **2 tbs curry powder**
- **4 cups assorted vegetables cut into 1 inch pieces**
- **2 large potatoes, cubed**
- **⅓ cup evaporated milk**
- **1 tbs chopped cilantro (chadon beni)**

● Heat the oil in a large saucepan. Add the onion, garlic and ginger and cook until fragrant.

● Mix the curry powder with ¼ cup water and add to the pan. Cook until almost dry then add the vegetables and combine, adding about ½ cup water. Season with salt and freshly ground black pepper, cover and simmer, stirring to prevent the vegetables sticking and adding more water if necessary.

● When the vegetables are tender, about 15 minutes, add the evaporated milk and cilantro. Stir and cook for a few minutes more.

● Serve immediately.

Serves 4–6

Sensational Pumpkin Gratin

- **2 lb pumpkin, peeled and cut into 1 inch chunks**
- **2 tbs vegetable oil**
- **1 large onion, finely chopped**
- **2 garlic cloves, chopped**
- **2 pimento peppers, seeded and chopped**
- **½ hot pepper, seeded and chopped**
- **½ cup chopped fresh herbs**
- **2 tbs flour**
- **1 cup vegetable stock**
- **1 cup milk**
- **½ tsp grated nutmeg**

FOR THE GRATIN
- **½ cup dry bread crumbs**
- **1 tbs olive oil**
- **½ cup grated cheese**
- **¼ cup chopped parsley**

- Preheat the oven to 375°F. Lightly butter a baking dish.
- Steam the pumpkin for about 6–8 minutes, until cooked but firm.
- Heat the oil in a saucepan and add the onion, garlic, peppers and herbs. Sauté until fragrant.
- Add the flour and cook for a few minutes.
- Combine the stock with the milk. Add to the pot and stir until thick. Season with salt, freshly ground black pepper and the nutmeg.
- Place the pumpkin in the prepared dish and pour the sauce over.
- Combine all the gratin ingredients and sprinkle onto the pumpkin.
- Bake for about 15 minutes until bubbling.

Serves 6

Melongene Cake with Tomato Sauce

This is a French Caribbean dish.

- 2 lb eggplant (melongene)
- 1 tbs salt
- 2 tbs vegetable oil
- 2 garlic cloves, minced
- ½ cup milk
- 3 eggs
- 1 tsp pepper sauce
- ⅓ cup chopped parsley

• Preheat oven to 325ºF.
• Wash, peel and cut the eggplant into strips. Sprinkle with the salt and let stand for 15 minutes. Wash and pat dry.
• Heat the oil in a sauté pan, add the garlic and cook without burning. Add the eggplant and cook until tender, about 20 minutes. Purée and set aside.
• Combine the milk with the eggs. Add the eggplant and stir. Mix in the pepper sauce and parsley.
• Turn into a greased baking dish. Place the baking dish into a larger dish filled with about 1 inch of water.
• Bake for 40 minutes until firm.
• Remove from oven, turn into a serving platter and pour over the tomato sauce.

Serves 4–6

Tomato Sauce

- 2 tbs olive oil
- 4 garlic cloves, finely chopped
- 2 onions, finely chopped
- 28 oz can whole tomatoes, puréed
- 1 tsp tomato paste
- ½ tsp salt
- ¼ cup chopped fresh basil
- 1 cup chicken stock
- 2 tsp brown sugar

• Heat the oil. Add the garlic and onions and sauté for about 3–5 minutes.
• Add the tomatoes, tomato paste, salt, freshly ground black pepper and basil. Add the stock and sugar. Stir and simmer for 40 minutes until thick.
• Taste and adjust seasoning. Serve with the melongene cake.

Makes about 3 cups

Green Fig Pie

- **12 green figs**
- **½ cup milk**
- **2 tbs butter**
- **½ cup grated cheese**
- **⅓ cup bread crumbs**

- Boil the figs in plenty of water. Peel and crush with a potato crusher.
- Using an electric mixer, add the milk and butter to the figs and beat until smooth (you may need a little more milk). Mix in some of the cheese and season with salt and freshly ground black pepper. Place in an ovenproof dish.

- Preheat broiler or grill.
- Combine the crumbs with a little salt and the rest of the cheese. Sprinkle onto the figs and broil until golden.

Serves 4

Oven-baked Plantain in Rum & Orange Juice

- **2 plantains (almost ripe)**
- **½ cup orange juice**
- **1 tbs rum**
- **1½ tsp ground cinnamon**

- Preheat oven to 375ºF.
- Peel and slice plantains lengthways and place in a well-greased ovenproof dish.

- Mix the orange juice with the rum and pour over the plantains. Sprinkle with cinnamon.
- Bake for 15 minutes until tender, turning once if necessary.

Serves 4

Curried Seim & Pigeon Peas

Seim is a bean similar to a green bean, which has peas inside the pods. They do need more cooking time than green beans and cannot be eaten raw.

- 1 tbs vegetable oil
- 1 onion, thinly sliced
- 2 garlic cloves, chopped
- 1 hot pepper, seeded and chopped
- 2 tbs curry powder mixed with ⅓ cup water
- 1 lb fresh seim, stringed and cut into 1 inch pieces
- 1 tomato, chopped
- 1 cup cooked pigeon peas

• Heat the oil in a sauté pan and add the onion, garlic and pepper. Cook until fragrant and the onion begins to turn brown. Add the curry paste and cook until the water has evaporated.

• Add the seim and tomato and stir to combine. Add the pigeon peas and stir, adding a small amount of water.

• Cover and cook for about 30 minutes until tender, stirring occasionally and only adding water when necessary.

Serves 4–6

Eggplant in Yogurt Sauce

- ¼ cup olive oil
- 1 medium eggplant, sliced into ½ inch slices
- 1 medium onion, sliced
- 1 cup plain yogurt
- 2 garlic cloves, minced
- 1 tbs chopped fresh mint or parsley

- Heat the oil in a shallow frying pan and fry the eggplant slices until golden brown. Drain.
- Pan fry the onion until translucent. Remove.
- Preheat oven to 350ºF. Grease a shallow casserole dish.
- Combine the yogurt with the garlic, mint, and salt and freshly ground black pepper.
- Arrange the eggplant slices in overlapping rows in the dish. Add the onions, pour the yogurt mixture over and bake for 10–15 minutes until bubbling.

Serves 4–6

Pea & Vegetable Curry

- **6 garlic cloves**
- **1 onion, chopped**
- **1 inch piece of ginger**
- **1 tbs vegetable oil**
- **1 tsp ground cumin (geera)**
- **1 tsp ground coriander**
- **1 tsp saffron powder**
- **1 cinnamon stick**
- **⅔ cup tinned tomatoes, crushed**
- **1 hot pepper, seeded and chopped**
- **14 oz can or 1½ cups cooked pigeon peas**
- **1 cup bodi or green beans, cut into 1 inch pieces**
- **1 cup cauliflower segments**
- **1 carrot, chopped**
- **1 potato, peeled and cubed**
- **1 bell pepper, seeded and chopped**

- Place the garlic, onion and ginger into a blender. Add ¼ cup water and blend to a smooth paste.
- Heat the oil in large sauté pan. Add the paste from the blender and cook until light brown in color. Add the dried spices and cook for 2 more minutes.
- Add the tomatoes and hot pepper and stir well. Add the pigeon peas and fresh vegetables. Stir well to combine.
- Cover and cook for about 20 minutes, stirring occasionally and adding just a small amount of water to prevent sticking.
- Serve with a fresh salad and steamed rice.

Serves 4–6

Eastern Style Pigeon Peas

- **1 large onion**
- **1 inch piece of ginger**
- **2 tbs vegetable oil**
- **1 tsp cumin seeds**
- **1 tsp garlic**
- **1 tsp ground cumin (geera)**
- **1 tsp chili powder**
- **1 tsp ground coriander**
- **½ tsp turmeric or saffron powder**
- **2 cups cooked pigeon peas**
- **1 cup sliced mushrooms**
- **⅓ cup puréed tomatoes**
- **½ cup evaporated milk**
- **2 tbs chopped cilantro (chadon beni)**

- Purée the onion with the ginger.
- Heat the oil in a sauté pan. Add the cumin seeds and cook until they sizzle. Add the onion and ginger purée with the garlic; stir and cook this mixture until it begins to brown.
- Add the ground cumin, chili powder, coriander and turmeric. Stir well and cook for a few seconds more.
- Add the pigeon peas and stir, followed by the mushrooms. Stir, cook for a few seconds, then add the tomatoes. Cook for about 2 minutes, add the evaporated milk and cover.
- Simmer, stirring occasionally, until the mixture becomes thick, about 10 minutes. Add a little water or broth to prevent sticking if necessary.
- Add the cilantro and season to taste with salt and freshly ground black pepper. You should finish with a thick mixture with only a little sauce.

Serves 4

Pumpkin Pancakes

Serve these with roasted or stewed meats.

- **1 cup cooked pumpkin, mashed**
- **1 egg**
- **¼ cup sugar**
- **1 tsp ground cinnamon**
- **¼ tsp grated nutmeg**
- **1 tsp baking powder**
- **1 cup all-purpose flour**
- **vegetable oil for frying**

- Combine the pumpkin and the egg. Add all the dry ingredients and stir until just combined.
- Brush a non-stick frying pan with a little oil and drop the batter by tablespoonfuls into the pan. Cook until the mixture is set and bubbles form at the top side.
- Flip the pancakes over and cook until browned on the other side.
- Remove from the pan and sprinkle with extra cinnamon and sugar, if desired.

Serves 4–6

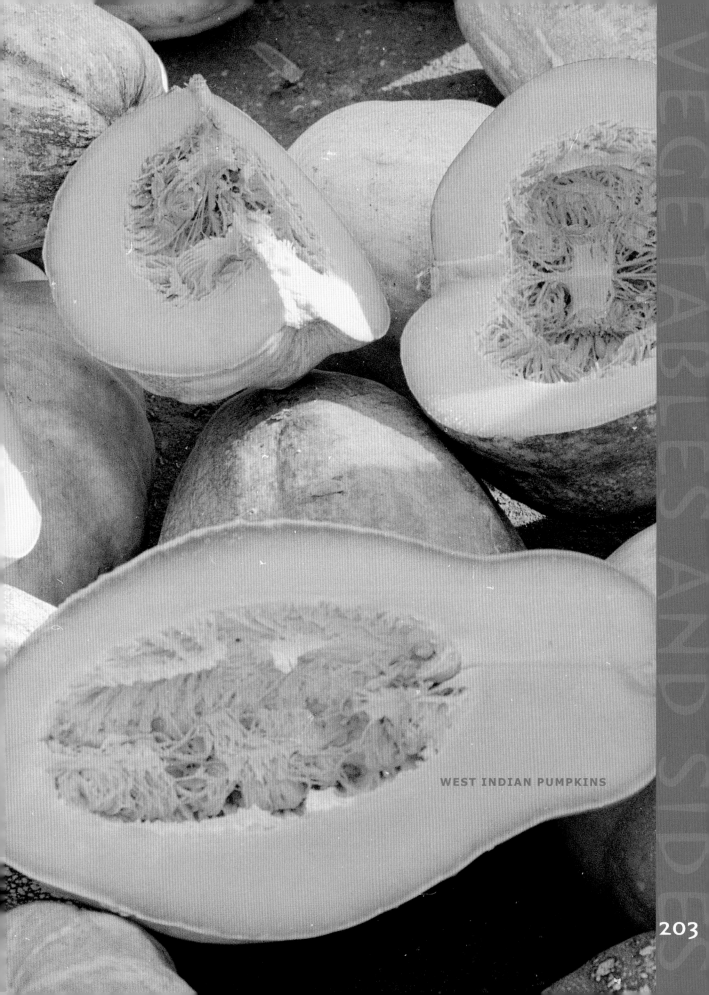

WEST INDIAN PUMPKINS

Creole Okra

- **1 tbs vegetable oil**
- **½ cup chopped onion**
- **½ cup chopped celery**
- **½ cup chopped peppers**
- **1½ cups chopped ochroes (okra)**
- **14 oz can corn niblets, drained**
- **8 oz can whole tomatoes, crushed with their juice**
- **1 tbs fresh thyme**
- **1 tsp paprika**
- **1 tsp cayenne pepper or 1 hot pepper, seeded and chopped**

● Heat the oil in a sauté pan and add the onion, celery and peppers. Cook for about 4 minutes until fragrant and tender.

● Add the ochroes, corn and tomatoes, and stir to combine. Add the thyme, paprika and cayenne or hot pepper and season with salt and freshly ground black pepper.

● Cook for about 30 minutes until the vegetables are tender.

Serves 4–6

Tasty Corn Cakes

- **1½ cups cornmeal**
- **1½ cups hot water**
- **1 cup grated cheese**
- **4 tbs melted butter**
- **1½ cups corn niblets**
- **½ cup chopped chives**
- **¼ cup chopped cilantro (chadon beni)**
- **1 tsp salt**
- **oil for frying**

- Combine all the ingredients to make a thick batter.
- Heat the oil in a frying pan and drop the batter by tablespoons into the pan. Using the back of a spoon, flatten the cakes. Pan fry for about 4 minutes per side, until golden brown.

Makes about 12–16

Oven-fried Fries

- **1½ lb potatoes, peeled and cut into wedges**
- **1 tsp chili powder**
- **1 tbs vegetable oil**
- **salt and freshly ground black pepper**

- Preheat oven to 375ºF.
- Place the potatoes in a bowl. Add all the other ingredients and rub onto the potato pieces.
- Place on a greased baking tray and bake, turning occasionally, for 20 minutes.

Serves 4–6

Spinach in Coconut Milk

- **1 large bunch young spinach**
- **2 tbs vegetable oil**
- **2 garlic cloves, chopped**
- **1 small onion, chopped**
- **1 hot pepper, seeded and chopped**
- **1 cup coconut milk**

- Wash and pick the spinach over and chop.
- Heat the oil in a sauté pan, add the garlic, onion and hot pepper and cook until translucent, about 3–5 minutes.
- Add the coconut milk, about a third at a time. Cover and simmer for about 10–15 minutes until tender, adding a little more coconut milk if necessary to prevent sticking.

Serves 4

Bok Choy
in Oyster Sauce

- **2 tbs oyster sauce**
- **½ tsp cornstarch**
- **1 tsp sesame oil**
- **1 bunch bok choy, washed**
- **1 tbs vegetable oil**
- **1 small onion, sliced**
- **2 garlic cloves, chopped**

• Combine the oyster sauce with the cornstarch and sesame oil and set aside.

• If not using baby bok choy, cut the bok choy into 1 inch pieces.

• Heat the vegetable oil in a wok, add the onion and garlic and sauté until fragrant.

• Add the bok choy and sprinkle with salt. Cook uncovered until water seeps from the bok choy. Add the sauce and cook just until the liquid is thick. Take care not to overcook or the bok choy will lose its bright green color.

Serves 4–6

Curried Green Figs

- **1 tbs vegetable oil**
- **1 onion, chopped**
- **2 garlic cloves, chopped**
- **½ hot pepper, seeded and chopped**
- **1 tbs curry powder**
- **1 lb green figs, peeled and cut into 1 inch pieces**
- **1 cup coconut milk**
- **2 tbs chopped cilantro (chadon beni)**

• Heat the oil in a sauté pan and add the onion, garlic and pepper. Sauté until the onion is almost browned.

• Mix the curry powder with ¼ cup water and add to the onion. Cook until dried.

• Add the green figs, turning well to coat with the curry mixture. Add the coconut milk, stir and bring to a boil. Season with salt and freshly ground black pepper.

• Turn the heat down low, cover and cook until the figs are tender, about 20–30 minutes.

• Serve sprinkled with the chopped cilantro.

Serves 4

Pigeon Pea Patties

- **1 tbs olive oil**
- **1 onion, chopped**
- **1 garlic clove, chopped**
- **1 large potato, boiled**
- **14 oz can pigeon peas**
- **1 tbs thyme**
- **1 tbs chopped chives**
- **⅓ cup chopped fresh basil**
- **½ hot pepper, seeded and chopped**
- **1 cup dry bread crumbs**
- **1 egg**
- **¼ cup vegetable oil**

- Heat the olive oil in a small frying pan, add the onion and garlic and cook until tender, about 3–4 minutes.
- In a large mixing bowl mash the potato well until very creamy – this will help the patty to hold together.
- Add the pigeon peas and the onion and garlic from the pan. Add the thyme, chives, basil and pepper.
- Stir well to combine. Season to taste with salt and freshly ground black pepper. Form the mixture into approximately 10 balls and set aside.
- Place the bread crumbs on a plate and season with salt and pepper. Lightly beat the egg.
- Flatten the mixture into patties about 2½ inches in diameter. Dip into egg and dredge in crumbs.
- Heat the vegetable oil in a frying pan and fry the patties until golden on both sides.
- Drain on paper towels. Serve warm as a side dish or as a main dish with a fresh salad and bread.

Makes 8–10

PIGEON PEAS

213

desserts

The best part of any meal, many would say! Caribbean desserts have evolved from cake and ice cream to the many exotic concoctions offered by great chefs throughout our islands. Of course simple fresh fruit can be the perfect ending to a meal, but our succulent, sweet and exotic fruits can also be transformed to become the main attraction, as in many of the following recipes, most of which can be lightened up, if preferred, by substituting low fat cream and cream cheeses. Passion fruit purée is used to give its distinct flavor both to a souffléd crêpe and to an ice cream. Pineapples are grilled with brown sugar and rum and are paired with papaya in a terrific fruit crumble. Mangoes are caramelized, spiced with cardamom in a mango tatin, and also puréed and made into a mousse. Bananas are caramelized, wrapped in crêpes and served with a rummy custard. Coconut is paired with chocolate to make a frozen mousse topped with a caramel rum sauce and is also used in a tropical crème brûlée. And finally limes star both in a Caribbean black-bottomed lime tart and in a refreshing lime mousse.

Grilled Pineapple
with Brown Sugar & Rum

There's something to be said about grilling fresh pineapple –
the fruit becomes succulent and juicy, absorbing all the flavors
it is infused with.
Serve with ice cream, or on its own for a
perfect fat-free dessert!

- **1 large pineapple**
- **½ cup brown sugar**
- **¼ cup dark rum**
- **1 tsp aromatic bitters**

- Preheat broiler. Line a shallow baking sheet or dish with foil.
- Peel the pineapple, remove eyes, then cut into half lengthways. Now cut these lengths into eight and remove the center core.
- Place the pineapple into the prepared dish and sprinkle with the sugar, rum and bitters.
- Broil until the pineapple turns brownish and the sugar starts to bubble and caramelize.
- Serve warm either on its own or with ice cream.

Serves 6–8

Mocha Dream Pie

This is a delicious alternative to the traditional mocha pie, which is much richer and sweeter.

- 1½ tbs gelatin
- 2 tbs instant coffee granules (extra strong)
- 2 eggs
- 1 cup granulated sugar
- 2 x 8 oz packages cream cheese
- 2 cups whipped cream
- 1 tbs cocoa powder
- chocolate shavings and chocolate chips to garnish

FOR THE CRUST
- 2 tablespoons sugar
- ⅓ cup butter, melted
- 2 cups graham cracker or chocolate cookie crumbs

- Preheat oven to 325ºF.
- To make the crust: add the sugar and butter to the crumbs and blend together or process in a food processor for a few seconds. Press into the bottom of a 10 inch pie plate and bake for 5 minutes until just firm. Leave to cool.
- Prepare the filling. Sprinkle the gelatin in 2 tablespoons of warm water and gently warm until dissolved.
- Combine the coffee with ½ cup hot water and stir into the gelatin mixture.
- Beat the eggs with the sugar, add to the gelatin mixture and cook over low heat for about 5 minutes until thick. Remove and leave to cool.
- Beat the cream cheese until smooth, add the egg and gelatin mixture and stir to combine. Fold in the whipped cream.
- Spoon into the prepared crust and chill overnight until firm.
- Place the cocoa powder into a strainer and sift over the cake. Arrange chocolate chips around the edge and sprinkle with chocolate shavings. Chill before serving.

Serves 8–10

For a lighter dish
Use low fat cream cheese and low fat whipped cream.

DESSERTS

Flan au Coco

This coconut flan is a French Caribbean speciality. Use freshly made coconut milk for the best flavor.

- 1⅓ cups granulated sugar
- 4 eggs
- 1 cup coconut milk
- 1 tsp vanilla extract
- 1 tsp lime zest
- 1 cup whole milk

- Preheat oven to 325°F.
- To make the caramel: combine 1 cup sugar with ¼ cup water in a saucepan. Stir and bring to a boil, then cook until the mixture turns a caramel color. Pour into 6 ramekin dishes.
- Beat the eggs with the coconut milk, vanilla, lime zest, milk and the remaining sugar until well blended. Strain the mixture.
- Pour the flan mixture into the caramel-lined dishes, place into a large baking tray and half-fill the tray with water.
- Bake until firm, about 30–35 minutes. Remove from the oven and refrigerate.
- To serve, invert onto individual plates.

Serves 6

Passion Pie

- 4 eggs, separated
- 1 cup sugar
- 2 tbs cornstarch
- 1 cup evaporated milk
- ½ cup passion fruit purée
- 1 pre-baked pie shell
- ¼ tsp cream of tartar

- In a small saucepan combine the egg yolks with ¾ cup sugar and the cornstarch. Add the evaporated milk and cook until the mixture becomes thick. Remove from heat and stir in the passion fruit purée. Pour into the pie shell and chill.
- Preheat oven to 325°F.
- Beat the egg whites with the remaining sugar and the cream of tartar until stiff. Spoon onto the pie and bake until lightly browned, about 15 to 20 minutes.
- Serve with a dollop of whipped cream.

Serves 6–8

Banana Fritters with Pomegranate Brown Sugar Cane Syrup

The slight sourness of the pomegranate syrup balances the sweetness of the fritters and adds an exotic twist to a traditional dish.

- **vegetable oil for deep frying**
- **4 bananas, sliced diagonally into 1 inch slices**
- **confectioners' sugar**

FOR THE BATTER
- **1 cup flour**
- **2 tsp sugar**
- **½ tsp baking powder**
- **1 egg**
- **½ cup milk**

FOR THE SYRUP
- **½ cup brown sugar**
- **3 tbs pomegranate molasses**
- **1 inch piece of cinnamon stick**

- To make the batter: combine all the ingredients and whisk to a smooth consistency. Refrigerate for 30 minutes or so until ready for use.
- To make the syrup: combine the sugar with ⅓ cup water in a small saucepan. Add the cinnamon and boil until thick, about 10 minutes. Remove the cinnamon stick and stir in the pomegranate molasses. Leave to cool.
- Heat the oil in a deep pan, cover the banana pieces with the batter and deep fry for about 3 minutes per side until golden.
- Drain, dust with confectioners' sugar and serve immediately with the syrup.

Serves 4–6

Passion Fruit Souffléd Crêpes

These soufflé crêpes are redolent with the distinct and flowery flavor of passion fruit. Make sure you serve them right away as they do deflate very quickly!

- confectioners' sugar

FOR THE CRÊPES
- ½ cup all-purpose flour
- ¼ tsp grated nutmeg
- 1 tbs sugar
- ¼ cup milk
- 1 tbs rum
- 1 tsp vanilla extract
- 1 egg and 1 egg yolk
- 1½ tbs melted butter

FOR THE SOUFFLÉ
- 4 eggs, separated
- ⅔ cup granulated sugar
- 1 cup evaporated milk
- 1 tsp vanilla extract
- ⅓ cup passion fruit purée
- ¼ tsp cream of tartar

- To make the crêpes: place the flour, nutmeg and sugar in a mixing bowl. Whisk in the milk, ¼ cup water, the rum and the vanilla until smooth. Add the egg and yolk and continue whisking until smooth. Add the melted butter and combine. Cover and rest for 1 hour in the refrigerator.
- Heat a non-stick frying pan and pour in ¼ cup crêpe batter. Tilt the pan and distribute the batter so that it covers the base of the pan completely. Pour off any excess batter.
- Cook until the batter is almost transparent. Flip over when bubbles appear, cook for a few seconds more and remove. Repeat for the remaining batter. This amount of batter should make 6 crêpes.
- To make the passion fruit soufflé: beat the egg yolks with half the sugar, add the evaporated milk and vanilla and warm over a low heat until thick. Remove and stir in the passion fruit purée.
- Beat the egg whites with the cream of tartar until frothy, add the rest of the sugar and beat to soft peak stage.
- Add some of the egg white to the cooled custard, then add the custard mixture to the egg white and fold to incorporate.
- Just before serving: preheat oven to 400ºF.
- Place the crêpes onto a greased baking tray or ovenproof dish, spoon some soufflé onto half of each crêpe, fold over and place in the oven. Cook until lightly browned and puffed, about 5 minutes.
- Remove from oven, dust with confectioners' sugar and serve immediately.

Serves 6

Caribbean Lime Mousse

Fast, fresh and definitely refreshingly light,
a true taste of the Caribbean.

- **1½ cups sugar**
- **⅓ cup cornstarch**
- **pinch of salt**
- **4 eggs, separated**
- **1 tsp vanilla extract**
- **⅓ cup fresh lime juice**
- **¼ cup evaporated milk**

GARNISH
- **1 tbs lime zest, chopped**
- **dash of aromatic bitters**

- Heat 1⅔ cups water in a saucepan. Whisk in the sugar, cornstarch and salt and stir until the mixture thickens.
- Beat the egg yolks in a bowl with the vanilla. Add a spoonful of the hot liquid to the eggs, then add the egg mixture to the hot liquid in the pan and stir constantly over a low heat for 2 minutes. Add the lime juice and milk. Leave the mixture to cool.
- Beat the egg whites to stiff peaks and fold into the lime custard.
- Spoon into stemmed glasses, garnish with chopped lime zest and top with a dash of aromatic bitters.

Serves 4

*For a lighter dish
Use low fat milk.*

225

Coconut Crème Brûlée

- **4 eggs**
- **1 cup coconut milk**
- **1 tsp vanilla extract**
- **1 tsp lime zest**
- **1 cup whole milk**
- **⅓ cup granulated sugar**
- **½ cup soft brown sugar**

- Preheat oven to 325°F.
- Beat the eggs with the coconut milk, vanilla, lime zest, milk and sugar until well blended. Strain the mixture.
- Pour the flan mixture into individual dishes, place into a large baking tray and half-fill the tray with water.
- Bake until firm, about 45 minutes.
- Remove and refrigerate until thoroughly chilled.
- Preheat broiler.
- Spoon the brown sugar over the tops of the coconut custards to cover and broil until the sugar is melted.
- Chill in the refrigerator before serving.

Serves 6

Mango Fool

- ¼ cup rum
- 2 tsp gelatin
- ½ cup evaporated milk
- 1 egg
- ½ cup granulated sugar
- 1 tsp lime zest, minced
- 1 cup chopped mango
- 1 cup whipping cream
- sprigs of mint to garnish

• Heat the rum gently. Remove from the heat and stir the gelatin into the rum to dissolve. Set aside to cool.
• Bring the milk to a boil. Remove from the heat.
• Whisk the egg with the sugar. Add a little of the hot milk to the mixture, stir, then return this to the milk in the pan.
• Cook slowly until thick and the mixture coats the back of a spoon, about 2 minutes.
• Stir in the gelatin mixture and lime zest and cook for about 1 minute more.
• Strain the custard, add the mango and stir. Cool in the refrigerator until cold but not set.
• Beat the whipping cream to stiff peaks and gently fold into the cooled mango custard.
• Pipe or spoon into stemmed glasses, cover and refrigerate until ready for serving.
• Garnish with sprigs of fresh mint and chopped fresh mango.

Serves 4

DESSERTS

Sticky Pudding
with Caramel Sauce

FOR THE SAUCE
- ½ cup unsalted butter
- 2 cups brown sugar
- 4 cups whipping cream
  or evaporated milk

FOR THE CAKE
- ¾ cup rum
- 1½ cups chopped dried fruit
- 1 tsp baking soda
- 1 cup unsalted butter
- ⅔ cup sugar
- 4 eggs
- 2 tsp vanilla extract
- 2½ cups all-purpose flour
- 2 tsp baking powder

- To make the sauce: melt the butter in a saucepan, add the brown sugar and cream or milk and bring to a boil. Cook until the sugar is melted, then cook on a low heat until the sauce has thickened and reduced, about 15 minutes.
- Preheat oven to 350ºF. Grease and flour a 12-cup cake pan.
- To make the cake: place the rum, ¾ cup water and the dried fruit in a saucepan. Add the baking soda and boil for 2 minutes. Remove and leave to cool.
- Cream the butter and sugar until light and fluffy. Add the eggs one at a time.
- Add the vanilla to the fruits.
- Combine the flour with the baking powder. Fold the flour and the fruits alternately into the creamed mixture in three additions, beginning and ending with the flour. Put the mixture into the prepared cake pan.
- Bake for 45 minutes, remove from the oven, pour on ¾ cup caramel sauce and bake for another 15 minutes.
- Remove from oven, cool and serve with the remaining sauce.

Serves 10–12

For a lighter dish
Use low fat cream or milk.

Sponge Roll with Papaya-Lime Curd

Papaya and lime are two fruits that blend beautifully together – and not only does this dessert taste great, it's very pretty too!

- **4 eggs**
- **1 cup granulated sugar**
- **1 inch strip of lime peel**
- **1 cup all-purpose flour**
- **½ tsp baking powder**
- **confectioners' sugar**

FOR THE PAPAYA-LIME CURD
- **1 cup papaya purée**
- **½ cup sugar**
- **⅓ cup butter**
- **1 tbs fresh lime juice**
- **1 tbs grated lime zest**
- **1 egg yolk, lightly beaten**

- To make the curd: place the papaya in a saucepan and stir in the sugar, butter, lime juice and lime zest. Cook gently to combine all the ingredients.
- Cool a little, then stir in the egg yolk and cook until thickened. Refrigerate for at least 4 hours or overnight.
- Preheat the oven to 350°F.

- Make the sponge. Beat the eggs with the sugar and lime peel until thick and ribbons form from the beaters when lifted, about 5 minutes. Add 2 tablespoons of water and fold in the flour and baking powder.
- Spread the batter into a lined, greased and floured baking tray and bake for 15–20 minutes until the cake springs back when touched.
- Remove from oven, place a clean tea towel on a wire rack and sprinkle with confectioners' sugar.
- Turn out the cake onto the towel and carefully remove the lining paper. Trim away any hard edges, then roll up the cake starting at the short end. Cool for 30 minutes.
- Unroll and spread with papaya-lime curd. Roll up again and refrigerate until ready to serve.
- Slice and serve with a dollop of thick cream if desired.

Serves 10

Passion Fruit & Pistachio Nut Ice Cream

- **pulp of 8 passion fruits (see method)**
- **⅓ cup shelled pistachio nuts, chopped**
- **½ cup milk**
- **1½ cups cream**
- **6 egg yolks**
- **1¼ cups granulated sugar**
- **2 inch strip of lime peel**

- To pulp passion fruit, cut the fruit in half, scoop out the seeds and pass through a food mill.
- Lightly toast the nuts in a preheated 250ºF oven just until fragrant, about 3–5 minutes. Remove and cool.
- Heat the milk with the cream in a saucepan until almost boiling. Cool slightly.
- With an electric beater beat the yolks, sugar and lime peel until pale and thick. Add some of the milk and cream mixture, stirring constantly. Remove the lime peel.
- Add the egg mixture to the pan with the remaining milk mixture. Stir over medium heat until lightly thickened. Do not boil, or the eggs will curdle.
- Cool the mixture and stir in the passion fruit pulp.
- Pour the mixture into a metal tray (6-cup capacity). Freeze for 3–4 hours or until just frozen around the edges.
- Transfer the mixture to a large bowl and beat with electric beaters until thick and creamy. Add the pistachios, mix well and return to the freezer.
- Freeze overnight or until firm.

Serves 8

Ponche de Crème Ice Cream

Ponche de crème is a traditional drink, very similar to eggnog, served at Christmas time on the islands. This is a lovely ice cream flavored with rum and spices!

- **4 egg yolks**
- **½ cup granulated sugar**
- **2 cups whole or evaporated milk**
- **2 cups whipping cream**
- **¼ tsp grated nutmeg**
- **2 tbs grated orange zest**
- **¼ cup rum**

• Beat the egg yolks with the sugar until light and fluffy. Put in a saucepan with the milk and cook over a low heat until thick, being careful not to let it boil.

• Leave the mixture to cool.

• Lightly whip the cream and fold it into the chilled custard mixture. Add the nutmeg and orange zest and stir in the rum.

• Chill the mixture, then place in an ice cream maker. Process according to the manufacturer's instructions.

Makes about 6 cups

Pineapple Ice Cream

- **4 eggs**
- **1 cup granulated sugar**
- **2 cups milk**
- **1 tsp vanilla extract**
- **1 cup heavy cream**
- **1 cup crushed pineapple, drained**

- Beat the eggs with the sugar until thick. Heat the milk and combine with the sugar and eggs. Add the vanilla and return to the heat. Cook without boiling until the custard is thick and coats the back of a wooden spoon.
- Remove from the heat, strain and cool slightly.
- Add the cream and stir in the pineapple. Chill for 4 hours.
- Place in an ice cream maker and process according to the manufacturer's instructions.

Makes 4 cups

Piña Colada Sorbet

- ⅓ cup granulated sugar
- 14 oz fresh or canned pineapple chunks
- ½ cup fresh coconut milk
- ¼ cup dark rum
- 1 tablespoon fresh lime juice

- Place the sugar and ⅓ cup water into a small saucepan. Stir to dissolve and bring to a boil just until the sugar melts, about 1 minute. Remove from heat and cool. Refrigerate until cold.
- Place the pineapple and coconut milk into the bowl of a food processor and process just until the pineapple has been crushed into small pieces. Remove and refrigerate.
- Combine the pineapple and coconut mixture with the cold sugar syrup. Stir in the rum and lime juice.
- Pour the mixture into a 9 x 5 inch baking pan and freeze until firm, about 4–6 hours.
- Remove from freezer and process in a blender or food processor until smooth but not thawed.
- Place in a covered container and freeze.

Makes about 4½ cups or serves 8–9

Custard Tarts with Caramelized Roasted Pineapple

- 1 medium pineapple, cored, peeled and sliced into rings
- 1 tsp aromatic bitters
- 8 tbs brown sugar
- 1 batch flaky pastry (see below)
- 8 glacé cherries (optional)

FOR THE CUSTARD
- ⅓ cup granulated sugar
- 2 tbs cornstarch
- 2 eggs
- ½ cup milk

- To make the custard: combine the sugar with the cornstarch in a saucepan. Whisk in the eggs until light, pour in the milk and cook gently until thick, without boiling. Remove from the heat and leave to cool.
- Preheat broiler.
- Combine the pineapple with the bitters and 2 tablespoons of the sugar. Place into a greased pie plate.
- Put under the broiler and broil for 10 minutes, turning once, until golden and the sugar has caramelized.
- Preheat oven to 400ºF.
- Roll out the pastry to ¼ inch thickness, stamp out 4 inch circles, and place on a lined baking sheet.
- Spread about 1 tablespoon of the custard onto each pastry round, leaving about an inch uncovered around the edge. Place a pineapple ring onto the custard.
- Fold the pastry upwards and tuck onto the pineapple and custard so that the pineapple ring is left partially uncovered.
- Sprinkle with the remaining brown sugar. Place a cherry into the center if desired.
- Bake for 20 minutes until golden.

Makes 8

Flaky Pastry

- 2 cups all-purpose flour
- ¾ cup butter
- pinch of salt
- ⅓ cup ice water

- Combine the butter with the flour until the butter is the size of small peas. Add the ice water and bring together. Form into a ball and refrigerate for 1 hour or until needed.

DESSERTS

Old-fashioned Cheesecake

- **2 cups graham cracker crumbs**
- **4 tbs sugar**
- **⅓ cup butter, melted**

FOR THE FILLING
- **2 lb cream cheese, at room temperature**
- **1 cup granulated sugar**
- **4 tbs flour**
- **6 eggs**
- **1 tsp vanilla extract**
- **1 cup sour cream**

- Preheat oven to 325ºF.
- Make the crust by combining the crumbs with the sugar and melted butter. Press into the bottom and partly up the sides of a 9 or 10 inch springform pan. Bake for 5 minutes and remove.
- To make the filling: beat the cream cheese in a large mixing bowl until smooth. Add the sugar and flour and combine.
- Beat in the eggs one at a time until well combined and the mixture is smooth. Add the vanilla. Fold in the sour cream and pour over the crust.
- Bake for 50–60 minutes.
- Run a knife around the rim of the pan to loosen the cheesecake. Cool completely before removing from the pan.
- Chill for 4–6 hours before serving.

Serves 12–15

Tip
If using a springform pan, wrap the pan in foil during baking to prevent any liquid from dripping through the seam of the pan.

For a lighter dish
Use plain yogurt instead of sour cream and low fat cream cheese.

Banana Rum Puffs

Serve these drizzled with chocolate or caramel sauce.

- **1½ cups butter**
- **4 cups all-purpose flour**
- **pinch of salt**
- **1 cup thin yogurt or sour cream**

FOR THE FILLING
- **2 large bananas,**
  puréed or finely chopped
- **2 tsp fresh lime juice**
- **12 oz cream cheese**
- **½ cup sugar**
- **2 tbs rum**
- **1 tsp ground cinnamon**
- **2 egg yolks**

• Make the pastry. Place the butter, flour and salt in a work bowl and blend until the mixture resembles fine crumbs. Add the yogurt and blend or combine just until it holds together. Form into a ball and chill for 1 hour.

• To make the filling: combine the bananas and lime juice and set aside. Cream the cheese with the sugar until smooth. Add the rum, cinnamon and egg yolks and mix until smooth. Combine with the bananas.
• Preheat oven to 400°F.
• Divide the pastry into 6 pieces, and keep the dough you are not working with chilled.
• Take one piece of dough and roll out to ⅛ inch thickness. Cut into six 4 inch squares.
• Take a muffin tin and place a dough square over one muffin cup. Put about 1 tablespoon of filling into the center and ease the pastry into the cup, bringing the ends gently together.
• Repeat with all the dough. You should get about 36 puffs.
• Bake for 10–15 minutes until lightly browned. Serve warm.

Makes 36

Ginger Pineapple Tart

A variation on the custard and caramelized roasted pineapple tartlets (page 234), here the custard is infused with ginger and rum and the tart is drizzled with melted chocolate.

FOR THE CRUST
- ½ cup butter
- 1 cup all-purpose flour
- 1 tbs sugar
- 2 oz block chocolate or chocolate chips

FOR THE FILLING
- 1 cup milk
- 1 tsp grated ginger
- 3 egg yolks
- ⅓ cup sugar
- 1 tbs flour
- 1 tbs cornstarch
- 1 tbs rum
- ½ cup whipping cream

FOR THE TOPPING
- 1 cup chopped pineapple
- 2 tbs brown sugar
- 1 tbs rum
- splash of aromatic bitters
- melted chocolate (optional)

- To make the crust: combine the butter with the flour until the butter is the size of small peas. Add the sugar and a little cold water to bring together. Form into a ball and refrigerate for 1 hour.
- Preheat oven to 400ºF.
- Roll the pastry out to fit a 9 inch tart pan or pie plate. Place a piece of foil into the plate and add some dried beans to weight the pastry.
- Bake for about 15 minutes, remove foil and beans, then bake for 10 minutes more. Remove from the oven and leave to cool.
- Melt the chocolate gently in a saucepan. Stir to a creamy consistency, cool, then use to brush the bottom of the tart.
- To make the filling: heat the milk in a saucepan and add the ginger. Place the yolks with the sugar, flour and cornstarch in a mixing bowl and beat until light in color. Add a little of the warmed milk and stir, then return this mixture to the milk in the saucepan.
- Cook on a low heat until the mixture thickens. Do not boil. Remove from the heat, add the rum and strain. Leave to cool.
- Beat the whipping cream and fold into the custard. Spoon into the tart shell and return to the fridge for a few hours.
- To make the topping: preheat broiler. Combine the pineapple with the sugar, rum and bitters and broil for a few minutes until the sugar melts. Remove and leave to cool.
- Spoon the topping over the tart before serving. If wished, drizzle with melted chocolate.

Serves 6–8

DESSERTS

Spiced Papaya with Coconut Custard

FOR THE PAPAYA
- **3 lb half-ripe papaya**
- **1 cup sugar**
- **3 tbs fresh lime juice**
- **1 cinnamon stick**
- **2 cups water**

FOR THE CAKE
- **4 eggs**
- **1 cup sugar**
- **1 cup all-purpose flour**
- **½ tsp baking powder**
- **1 tsp vanilla extract**

FOR THE CUSTARD
- **1 cup milk**
- **1 cup coconut milk**
- **4 egg yolks**
- **¼ cup sugar**
- **1 piece lime peel**
- **¼ cup dark rum**

- To prepare the papaya: Peel and cut the papaya into 1 inch strips. Place in a saucepan along with the other ingredients and cook gently for 15–20 minutes until a thick syrup is formed. Remove and cool.
- Preheat oven to 350°F. Grease and line a 9 inch cake pan.

- To make the cake: beat the eggs with the sugar until thick, about 5 minutes. Add 2 tablespoons of water. Combine the flour and baking powder and fold into the egg mixture. Add the vanilla.
- Pour into the prepared pan and bake for 10–12 minutes. Remove from the oven and leave to cool.
- Use a cookie cutter to cut out 12 rounds, 2½ inches in diameter.
- To make the custard: heat the milk and coconut milk together. Beat the egg yolks with the sugar and lime peel.
- Add a little warmed milk to the sugar mixture, then add the sugar mixture to the milk in the saucepan and cook until thick. Add the rum and remove from the heat. Leave to cool.
- To assemble, place one sponge round onto a serving plate and spoon some papaya on top together with some spiced syrup. Top with some coconut custard.
- You may either serve it like this or add another sponge round to top it off, spooning more fruit and custard over.

Makes 12

Caribbean Pumpkin Flan with Burnt Orange Sauce

Pumpkin is available all year in the Caribbean and makes a delicious and rich-tasting flan that is balanced by the burnt orange sauce.

- **4 eggs**
- **½ cup granulated sugar**
- **⅛ cup flour**
- **1 tsp vanilla extract**
- **1 cup whole milk**

FOR THE PUMPKIN
- **2 cups grated raw pumpkin**
- **½ cup water**
- **¼ cup brown sugar**
- **2 tsp mixed spice (cinnamon, nutmeg, allspice, mace)**
- **½ tsp ground ginger**

- Combine all the ingredients for the pumpkin in a small saucepan, bring to a boil and simmer for 10 minutes until soft. Purée and set aside.
- Beat the eggs with the sugar, flour and vanilla. Add the milk and combine.
- Place in a small saucepan and cook until thick. Remove and strain. Leave to cool.
- Preheat oven to 350°F.
- Combine the custard with the pumpkin. Pour into a 9 inch pie plate and bake for 30 minutes until firm. Serve with the burnt orange sauce.

Serves 6–8

Burnt Orange Sauce

- **½ cup sugar**
- **⅔ cup orange juice**
- **1 tsp orange zest**

- Place the sugar and ⅛ cup water into a heavy saucepan and cook until the sugar has caramelized. Remove from the heat and add the orange juice and zest. Return to the heat and cook until thick and bubbly.
- Pour onto the cooked pumpkin flan before serving.

DESSERTS

Pineapple Papaya Crumble

**This is simply sublime when served with a scoop
of coconut ice cream!**

- **1 cup brown sugar plus 2 tsp**
- **3 cloves**
- **2 cinnamon sticks**
- **1 tsp aromatic bitters**
- **1 pineapple (about 4 lb), peeled
  and cut into 1 inch pieces**
- **1 half-ripe papaya (about 3 lb),
  peeled and cut into 1 inch pieces**

FOR THE TOPPING
- **⅔ cup unsalted butter**
- **2½ cups flour**
- **½ cup granulated sugar**

- Preheat oven to 350°F.
- Prepare the filling. Place the brown
sugar, spices, bitters and ½ cup water
in a heavy medium saucepan and
bring to a boil. Add the fruit and cook
on a low heat for about 10 minutes.
Remove the fruit. If the syrup is not
very thick you can return it to the
heat and cook until slightly thickened.
- Meanwhile, make the crumble
topping: combine the butter with the
flour until the mixture resembles fine
crumbs. Add the sugar and combine.
- Place the fruit and thickened syrup
into a large greased ovenproof dish.
Spoon the crumble on top to cover
the fruit and sprinkle with a little
brown sugar.
- Bake until hot and bubbling, about
35 minutes.

Serves 10–12

Mango Apple Cobbler

- **2 apples, peeled and cut into chunks**
- **2 half-ripe julie mangoes, peeled and cut into ½ inch pieces**
- **⅓ cup brown sugar**
- **2 tsp ground cinnamon**

FOR THE TOPPING
- **1½ cups flour**
- **½ cup rolled oats**
- **⅓ cup brown sugar**
- **1 tbs baking powder**
- **1 tsp grated nutmeg**
- **½ cup unsalted butter**
- **¾ cup milk**

- Preheat oven to 375ºF.
- Combine the apples, mangoes, sugar and cinnamon and place in a greased casserole dish.
- To make the topping: combine the flour, oats, sugar, baking powder and nutmeg. Cut the butter into the mixture until it resembles small peas. Add the milk and stir to a wet batter.
- Drop by spoonfuls onto the fruit and gently spread. It does not matter if the batter does not completely cover the fruit.
- Bake until bubbling, about 40–45 minutes.

Serves 6–8

Pineapple Cake

- ½ cup butter or margarine
- 1⅓ cups granulated sugar
- 2 large eggs
- ½ tsp grated lime zest
- 1 tsp vanilla extract
- 2 cups all-purpose flour
- 1 tsp baking soda
- ¾ tsp ground cinnamon
- pinch of salt
- 20 oz can crushed pineapple with juice
- confectioners' sugar

- Preheat oven to 350ºF. Butter and flour a 13 x 2 x 9 inch baking pan.
- With an electric mixer cream the butter with the sugar until light and fluffy. Add the eggs one at a time, beating well between additions. Add the lime zest and vanilla.
- Combine the flour, baking soda, cinnamon and salt. Sift twice and set aside.
- Add the flour mixture to the creamed mixture in three batches alternately with the pineapple in syrup, beginning and ending with the flour.
- Pour into the prepared pan and bake for 40 minutes or until a wooden toothpick comes out clean.
- Cool and dust with confectioners' sugar before serving.

Serves 12–15

Creamy Guava Tart

Stewed guava is a popular Caribbean dessert.
Here, stewed guavas are used with a custard to make an
exotic dessert.

- **12 guavas**
- **½ cup granulated sugar**
- **1 inch piece of cinnamon stick**

FOR THE CRUST
- **2 cups flour**
- **3 tbs sugar**
- **⅔ cup butter**
- **1 egg yolk**

FOR THE CUSTARD
- **2 egg yolks**
- **2 tbs sugar**
- **½ cup evaporated milk**
- **vanilla extract**

- Preheat oven to 375ºF.
- To make the crust: place the dry ingredients into a work bowl and cut the butter into the mixture until it resembles small peas. Add about ½ cup cold water and combine, using your hands to bring the dough together. Form into a ball and refrigerate for 30 minutes.
- Press the dough into the base and sides of a 10 inch tart pan with a removable base. Place a piece of foil into the tart pan to cover the pastry, then pour some dried peas into the shell.

- Bake for 10 minutes, remove foil and peas and bake for another 5–8 minutes. Remove from the oven. The tart shell should be cooked and slightly browned.
- To make the custard: beat the egg yolks with the sugar and evaporated milk. Add a little vanilla and stir.
- Peel the guavas, scoop out seeds, and pass the seeds and pulp through a food mill to remove the seeds. Set aside. Slice the guava peel.
- Place the guava peel and pulp into a small pan. Add the sugar, cinnamon and enough water to come halfway up the pan (some of the guavas will not be covered). Cook slowly until the fruit is tender, about 15–20 minutes. Leave to cool. Remove the piece of cinnamon.
- Spread the guavas over the base of the tart, then pour on the custard mixture. Bake for 30–35 minutes until golden and set.

Serves 6–8

DESSERTS

Guava Mousse

- **1 cup guava purée**
- **¼ cup rum or water**
- **juice of 2 limes**
- **⅓ cup granulated sugar**
- **1 tbs gelatin**
- **1 cup whipping cream**

• In a small saucepan combine half the guava purée with the rum or water, lime juice and sugar. Heat gently, then remove from heat, sprinkle on the gelatin and stir to dissolve without any lumps. Add the remaining guava purée and chill.

• Whip the cream and stir half into the chilled guava mixture, then gently fold in the rest.
• Spoon into dishes or cookie dough cups and refrigerate or freeze until ready for use.

Serves 4–6

Mango Mousse

- **¼ cup rum**
- **1 tbs gelatin**
- **1 cup mango pulp**
- **⅓ tsp lime zest, minced**
- **2 cups whipping cream**
- **sprigs of mint and chopped mango to garnish**

• Heat the rum gently, remove from the heat and stir in the gelatin to dissolve. Set aside to cool.
• Purée the mango in a food processor and add to the gelatin mixture with the lime zest. Stir well and refrigerate to cool.

• Beat the whipping cream to stiff peaks and gently fold into the mango mixture.
• Pipe into stemmed glasses, cover and refrigerate until ready for serving.
• Garnish with sprigs of fresh mint and chopped fresh mango.

Serves 4–6

Sapodilla Mousse

Sapodillas, also known as sapote, are one of my favorite fruits. The pulp or flesh is a rich brown with a pinkish hue.
It is soft and melts in your mouth. The flavor somewhat resembles pears infused with a rich maple syrup.

- **1 cup sapodilla purée**
- **⅓ cup granulated sugar**
- **¼ cup rum**
- **1 tbs gelatin**
- **1 cup whipping cream**

- Combine a quarter of the sapodilla purée with the sugar in a small saucepan. Heat gently to melt the sugar. Remove from the heat and leave to cool.
- Warm the rum. Sprinkle on the gelatin and stir to dissolve without any lumps.
- Add the remaining sapodilla purée together with the sapodilla and sugar mixture and chill.
- Whip the cream and stir half into the chilled sapodilla mixture, then gently fold in the rest.
- Spoon into dishes or cookie dough cups and refrigerate or freeze until ready for use.

Serves 4–6

Sapodilla Sorbet

- **1 cup sugar**
- **2 cups sapodilla purée**
- **¼ cup fresh lime juice**
- **¼ tsp crushed cardamom pods**

- Boil the sugar with 2 cups water until the sugar is dissolved. Leave to cool.
- Stir in the sapodilla purée, lime juice and cardamom.
- Pour into an ice cream maker and process according to the manufacturer's instructions.

Makes about 3 cups

Key Lime Cake

Do try this. It is a delicious cake with a sauce baked into it. Serve with whipped cream or ice cream.

- **3 tbs butter**
- **1 cup granulated sugar**
- **3 eggs, separated**
- **2 tsp lime zest**
- **¼ cup fresh lime juice**
- **1½ cups milk**
- **¼ cup flour**
- **¼ tsp salt**
- **¼ tsp cream of tartar**

- Preheat oven to 325ºF. Grease and flour a 9 x 9 inch cake pan.
- Cream the butter and sugar until fluffy. Add the egg yolks and blend until smooth. Combine the lime zest, lime juice and milk and stir into the creamed mixture alternately with the flour.
- Beat the egg whites until stiff with the salt and cream of tartar. Fold into the cake mixture.
- Pour the mixture into the prepared pan and place in a shallow pan filled with about 2 inches of water. Bake for about 1 hour.
- Cool before serving.

Serves 4–6

Caribbean Black-bottomed Lime Tart

This tart is light tasting and delicious, with the chocolate cookie crust adding a special flavor to the whole dish.

- 20 chocolate cookies
- 2 tbs chopped almonds
- 4 tbs melted butter

FOR THE FILLING
- 1 lb cream cheese
- ⅔ cup granulated sugar
- 2 eggs
- 1 tsp vanilla extract
- ½ cup sour cream
- 1½ tbs lime zest
- ¼ cup fresh lime juice

- Preheat oven to 350°F.
- Prepare the crust. Finely crush the cookies and almonds in a food processor. Add the melted butter and combine.
- Press the mixture into the bottom of a 9 inch pie plate. Refrigerate until ready for use.
- To make the filling: beat the cream cheese with an electric mixer until creamy. Add the sugar, eggs and vanilla and beat until smooth. Gently beat in the sour cream, lime zest and juice.
- Pour the mixture into the crust and bake for 40–50 minutes until the cheesecake is slightly puffed and the center is set.
- Refrigerate for 4 hours or overnight.

Serves 8–10

Sapodilla Pie

- **5 oz graham crackers**
- **1 tablespoon butter, melted**

FOR THE FILLING
- **¼ cup butter**
- **14 oz can condensed milk**
- **4 sapodillas, peeled, seeded and puréed**
- **¼ cup fresh lime juice**
- **1 tsp vanilla extract**
- **1 cup whipping cream**

- Preheat oven to 350ºF.
- Prepare the crust. Finely crush the graham crackers in a food processor, add the melted butter and combine.
- Press the mixture into the bottom of a 9 inch pie plate. Bake briefly for 5 minutes, remove from the oven and refrigerate.
- To make the filling: melt the butter in a small saucepan and add the condensed milk. Cook gently until the mixture becomes slightly golden. Remove and combine with the sapodilla purée, lime juice and vanilla. Let the mixture cool.
- Beat the cream with an electric mixer until fluffy.
- Fold the whipped cream into the sapodilla mixture. Pour into the pie crust and refrigerate for 4–6 hours or overnight, or freeze until ready for use.

Serves 6

Pineapple Ice Box Cake

This is a traditional dessert in Trinidad and Tobago
that has lost some appeal through the years, mainly through cooks
using inferior ingredients. Here I think I've managed to
breathe new life into it by simply going back to basics and using
pure and top quality ingredients.

- **5 eggs**
- **1 cup granulated sugar**
- **1 tsp vanilla extract**
- **1 inch strip of lime peel**
- **1 cup all-purpose flour**
- **confectioners' sugar**
- **¼ cup chopped toasted almonds**

FOR THE FILLING
- **½ cup unsalted butter**
- **1 cup sifted confectioners' sugar**
- **1 egg**
- **1 tsp vanilla extract**
- **2 cups heavy cream**
- **1½ cups crushed pineapple, drained**

- Preheat oven to 350°F.
- Beat the eggs with the sugar, vanilla and lime peel for about 5 minutes until thick and ribbons form from the beaters when lifted. Add 3 tablespoons of water. Fold in the flour.
- Spread batter into a greased and lined 10 x 5 inch baking tray and bake for 10–15 minutes, until the cake springs back when touched.
- Remove from oven, place a clean tea towel on a wire rack and sprinkle with confectioners' sugar. Turn out the cake onto the towel and carefully remove the lining paper.
- Line a loaf tin with plastic wrap and cut the cake to fit the base of the loaf tin. You will need 4 pieces.
- To make the filling: cream the butter with the confectioners' sugar until light and fluffy. Add the egg and beat until creamy. Stir in the vanilla.
- Place the cream in a small bowl and whip until light. Add 1½ cups to the butter mixture and combine. Fold in the pineapple.
- To assemble: place one layer of cake at the base of the loaf tin and spread a quarter of the pineapple filling over the cake. Repeat using 4 layers. Finish with the rest of the cream and sprinkle the almonds over the top.

Serves 10

DESSERTS

Crêpes with Caramelized Bananas & Rum Custard

- **6 bananas**
- **½ cup brown sugar**

FOR THE CRÊPES
- **1 cup cake flour**
- **½ cup milk**
- **1 tbs sugar**
- **1 tbs rum**
- **3 eggs**
- **¼ tsp salt**
- **2 tbs melted butter**

FOR THE CUSTARD
- **4 egg yolks**
- **2 cups evaporated milk**
- **¼ cup sugar**
- **2 tbs rum**
- **1 tsp vanilla extract**
- **½ tsp grated nutmeg**

- To make the crêpes: whisk together the flour, milk, sugar, rum and ½ cup water. Slowly stir in the eggs and add the salt. Whisk in the melted butter. Leave the mixture to rest for 10–30 minutes.
- Lightly grease a non-stick 4 inch frying pan or crêpe pan and cook the crêpes, using ¼ cup batter for each crêpe. Swirl the batter to cover the base of the pan, and when set flip over, cook for a few seconds more and remove.

Repeat until all the batter is used. This quantity should make 8–10 crêpes, 4 inches in diameter. Keep the crêpes warm while preparing the bananas and custard.
- Preheat broiler. Grease a shallow pie plate or baking tray.
- Peel the bananas and slice in two. Sprinkle with the sugar and broil until the bananas are caramelized, about 4–6 minutes. Remove and set aside.
- To make the custard: combine all the ingredients in a heavy saucepan and cook gently without boiling until the mixture thickens, about 5 minutes. Remove from the heat.
- To assemble: spoon the rum custard into the crêpes. Fold each crêpe over and top with one half of a caramelized banana. Serve with a dollop of whipping cream if desired.

Serves 10

256

Mango Tatin
with Cardamom & Lime

- **3 large half-ripe mangoes**
- **3 tbs butter**
- **1 cup granulated sugar**
- **½ tsp ground cardamom**
- **1 tbs fresh lime juice**

FOR THE PASTRY
- **1½ cups flour**
- **1 tbs granulated sugar**
- **6 tbs unsalted butter**
- **1 egg, beaten**

- To make the pastry: combine the flour, sugar and butter, rubbing the butter into the flour until the mixture resembles fine crumbs.
- Add the egg and bring the mixture together. If needed, dribble in a little cold water to help the mixture come together. Form into a ball and chill for 30 minutes.

- Preheat oven to 400ºF.
- Peel and pit the mangoes, and slice into uniform pieces.
- Melt the butter in a large ovenproof frying pan. Add the sugar and cardamom and cook until a caramel forms, about 5 minutes.
- Arrange the mango slices in a circular pattern onto the caramel and drizzle with the lime juice.
- Roll the pastry to fit the frying pan.
- Carefully cover the mangoes in the pan with the pastry, being sure to push the pastry down into the edges of the pan.
- Bake for 20 minutes until browned.
- Remove, run a knife around the rim of the pan to release the tart and immediately flip onto a platter.
- Leave to cool before serving.

Serves 8

Chocolate Coconut Mousse with Caramel Sauce

Here's a rich and dreamy frozen dessert made from chocolate and coconut mousse complemented by a warm caramel sauce.

- **1½ cups grated fresh coconut**
- **3 cups semi-sweet chocolate chips or 1½ lb semi-sweet chocolate**
- **2 cups whipping cream**
- **3 large egg yolks**
- **8 large egg whites, at room temperature**

FOR THE SAUCE
- **1¼ cups sugar**
- **1 cup whipping cream**
- **½ cup unsalted butter, cut into pieces**
- **¼ cup rum**
- **1 tsp vanilla extract**

- Lightly toast ½ cup grated coconut and set aside.
- Melt the chocolate in a small, heavy-based saucepan set in a larger pan of simmering water, stirring frequently.
- Add half the cream and the rest of the coconut and stir until creamy. Pour into a large bowl and cool. Chill the rest of the cream.
- Add the egg yolks to the cooled chocolate mixture and whisk well to combine.
- Beat the egg whites in a clean bowl until stiff but not dry.

- Whisk the rest of the cream in another bowl until soft peaks form. Fold the whipped cream into the chocolate mixture.
- Gently fold the beaten egg whites into the chocolate mixture.
- Pour the mixture into a 10 inch diameter springform pan. Cover and freeze overnight.
- To make the sauce: combine the sugar with ¼ cup water in a saucepan. Cook to boiling and continue to cook until the syrup turns to a caramel color. Avert your face to protect from any danger of getting burnt and add the cream very carefully as the mixture will bubble and splash vigorously.
- Remove from the heat and add the butter, rum and vanilla. Stir until smooth.
- Just before serving, remove the frozen mousse from the freezer and run a sharp knife around the edges. Release the pan sides.
- Cut the mousse into wedges, spoon warm caramel sauce onto individual plates and place a mousse wedge on top of the sauce.
- Sprinkle with the toasted coconut and serve.

Serves 8–10

cakes & breads

Almost always at any festive occasion in the Caribbean some type of cake will be served, be it a rich rum cake at Christmas or a sponge cake with a butter or egg white frosting at a birthday celebration.

This section includes some traditional favorites like fruited Dundee cake and chocolate cakes, made of course with our own local cocoa powder, which ranks among the best in the world. There are some delightful fresh fruit cakes and, of course, a wonderful sponge soaked with an orange-scented rum syrup, a celebration in taste! Last but not least, between these pages you'll find cakes redolent with our local spices from the spice isle of Grenada: cinnamon, nutmeg, allspice; and of course rum stars in many of the recipes. Breads form an integral part of the Caribbean diet and both sweet and savory breads are popular. We have rotis given to us by the Indians, bakes from the African and Creole influence, and European sweet breads and buns. They all carry a distinct Caribbean flavor: plantain bread, nutmeg muffins, stuffed paratha and coconut scones.

Here, in the delightful recipes that follow, we celebrate our Caribbean heritage.

Carrot Walnut Cake

Although carrot cake is not traditionally a Caribbean cake, we have adapted it and it has become very popular, especially on birthdays and other festive occasions.

- **4 eggs**
- **1½ cups sugar**
- **1 tsp vanilla extract**
- **1 cup vegetable oil**
- **2 cups sifted all-purpose flour**
- **2 tsp baking soda**
- **½ tsp salt**
- **2 tsp ground cinnamon**
- **½ tsp grated nutmeg**
- **¾ lb carrots, peeled and grated**
- **1 cup chopped walnuts**

- Preheat oven to 350ºF. Grease, line and flour a 9 x 13 inch cake pan or two 9 inch cake pans.
- Beat the eggs with the sugar until light and tripled in volume. Add the vanilla and, with beater on medium speed, slowly pour in the vegetable oil and beat for 1 minute.
- Sift together the dry ingredients.
- Reduce the beater speed to low and add the dry ingredients to the eggs, beating just until incorporated.
- Using a spatula, fold in the carrots and walnuts.
- Pour the batter into the prepared pan/pans.
- Bake for 45–50 minutes for the large cake or 35 minutes for the smaller cakes.
- Remove from oven, cool and frost.

Makes 1 rectangular cake or 2 round cakes

Cream Cheese Frosting

- **⅔ cup butter**
- **2½ cups confectioners' sugar, sifted**
- **1 lb cream cheese, at room temperature**
- **1 tbs milk**
- **1 tsp grated orange zest**

- Cream the butter with the confectioners' sugar until creamy. Add the cream cheese and stir until soft, adding a few drops of milk at a time if needed to form a spreadable consistency.
- Stir in the orange zest.
- Use to frost carrot walnut cake.

Rich West Indian Dundee Cake

- **1 lb butter**
- **½ lb granulated sugar**
- **½ lb brown sugar**
- **8 eggs**
- **zest of 3 limes**
- **2 tbs vanilla extract**
- **1 tsp almond extract**
- **1¼ lb all-purpose flour**
- **2 tsp baking powder**
- **2 oz ground almonds**
- **½ cup rum (optional)**
- **1 lb currants**
- **1 lb golden raisins**
- **½ lb candied citron peel**
- **¼ lb red and green candied cherries, chopped**
- **3 oz chopped nuts**

- Preheat oven to 325ºF. Grease and line 2 cake pans, 9 inches in diameter and 3 inches deep.
- Cream the butter and sugars until light and fluffy.
- Add the eggs one at a time, beating well between additions. Add the lime zest, vanilla and almond extract.
- Sieve the flour and baking powder and mix in the ground almonds.
- Fold into the batter, together with the rum if using.
- Toss the currants, golden raisins, peel, cherries and chopped nuts in some flour, coat evenly, then shake off excess flour. Add to the batter and gently fold in.
- Divide the mixture between the 2 prepared pans. Bake for about 1½ hours, or until the cake leaves the sides of the pan.
- Cool the cakes in the pans before removing.

Makes 2

Coconut Butter Cookies

**These delicious cookies are lightly flavored with coconut.
They are not too sweet and are perfect for tea time.**

- ¼ cup butter
- ½ cup sugar
- 1 egg
- ½ cup finely grated coconut
- ¼ tsp aromatic bitters
- 2 cups all-purpose flour
- 2 tsp baking powder
- ½ tsp baking soda
- ⅓ cup milk
- candied cherries to decorate

- Preheat oven to 375ºF.
- Cream the butter with the sugar. Add the egg and beat, then add the coconut and bitters.
- Combine the flour, baking powder and soda.
- Add the flour and the milk alternately to the creamed mixture. Stir to combine.
- Drop the batter by teaspoonfuls onto a greased baking sheet. Flatten slightly with a fork. Decorate with candied cherries.
- Bake for 10–15 minutes until lightly golden around the edges.

Makes about 20

Peppery Cornmeal Biscuits

- 1½ cups all-purpose flour
- ½ cup cornmeal
- 1 tbs baking powder
- 1 tbs sugar
- 1 tsp freshly ground black pepper
- pinch of salt
- 4 tbs softened butter
- ⅞ cup thin plain yogurt
- milk
- poppy seeds for sprinkling (optional)

- Preheat oven to 375ºF.
- Combine all the dry ingredients, then rub in the butter until the mixture is of a grainy texture. Add the yogurt and stir.
- Knead gently, turn onto a floured work surface and pat to a ¾ inch thickness.
- Cut out 3 inch circles and place on a baking sheet. Brush lightly with milk and sprinkle with poppy seeds if desired.
- Bake for 15 minutes until risen and cooked through.

Makes about 12

Nutty 'n' Fudgy Chocolate Cake

Cocoa is widely used on the islands in place of chocolate, and makes a great-tasting cake! This cake will keep for 2 days out of the refrigerator without the whipped cream.

- ⅔ cup butter
- 1¼ cups granulated sugar
- ⅓ cup cocoa powder
- 3 eggs, separated
- 2 cups flour
- 1 cup finely chopped walnuts
- 2 tsp baking powder
- 1 tsp vanilla extract
- 2 cups whipped cream
- confectioners' sugar

- Preheat oven to 350ºF. Line, grease and flour two 8 inch cake pans.
- Using an electric mixer, cream the butter with the sugar until light. Add the cocoa powder and beat for a few minutes to incorporate. Beat in the egg yolks.
- Combine the flour with the walnuts and baking powder.
- Fold this mixture into the butter and egg mixture alternately with ¾ cup water, adding the dry ingredients in three parts and the water in two, beginning and ending with the flour mixture.
- Beat the egg whites in a small bowl until soft peaks form. Fold lightly into the chocolate mixture.
- Spoon the batter into the prepared pans and bake for 35–40 minutes.
- Turn onto a wire rack to cool.
- Spoon whipped cream onto one cake, place the other cake on top, dust heavily with confectioners' sugar and serve, or slice the cakes as they are and serve whipped cream on the side.

Serves 8–10

Dark Chocolate Cake

- **1 cup boiling water**
- **¾ cup cocoa powder**
- **½ cup milk**
- **1 tsp vanilla extract**
- **2 cups all-purpose flour**
- **1¼ tsp baking soda**
- **pinch of salt**
- **1 cup butter**
- **1¼ cups brown sugar**
- **¼ cup granulated sugar**
- **4 eggs**

• Preheat oven to 350ºF. Either grease and line two 9 inch cake pans or line cupcake pans with paper cups.
• Whisk together the water, cocoa, milk and vanilla.
• Sift together the flour, baking soda and salt.
• Cream the butter and sugars in the mixing bowl of an electric mixer until light and creamy. Add the eggs one at a time, beating well between additions.
• Fold in the flour alternately with the liquid ingredients in three batches, beginning and ending with flour.
• Divide the batter between the prepared pans and bake 25–30 minutes for 9 inch cakes and 20–25 minutes for cupcakes. Cool, and top with brown sugar butter cream.

Makes 2 cakes or 24 cupcakes

Brown Sugar Butter Cream

- **3 egg whites**
- **½ tsp fresh lime juice**
- **1 tsp vanilla extract**
- **pinch of salt**
- **1 cup brown sugar**
- **1½ cups unsalted butter, soft but not at room temperature, cut into pieces**

• Place the egg whites, lime juice, vanilla and salt in a mixing bowl.
• Combine the brown sugar and ½ cup water in a saucepan and bring to a boil.
• Beat the egg whites until they just hold soft peaks.
• Meanwhile, allow the sugar to boil until a candy thermometer registers 238–242ºF.
• Remove from the heat and continue beating the eggs while you pour in the syrup in a steady stream.
• Add the butter a piece at a time and beat well. If the mixture becomes runny, refrigerate, then continue.
• Use to top chocolate cakes.

Banana Cake Spiced with Nutmeg & Cinnamon

- ½ cup milk
- ½ tbs lime juice
- 2 cups all-purpose flour
- 2 tsp baking soda
- 1 tsp baking powder
- 1 tsp ground cinnamon
- ¼ tsp grated nutmeg
- ¼ tsp salt
- 4 oz unsalted butter
- 1⅓ cups sugar
- 4 eggs
- 3 ripe bananas, mashed (1¼ cups)

• Preheat oven to 350ºF. Line and grease a round cake pan, 9 inches in diameter and 3 inches deep.
• Combine the milk and lime juice and let stand for 10 minutes until curdled.
• Sift the flour, baking soda, baking powder, spices and salt.
• Cream the butter with the sugar on medium speed until creamy. Add the eggs one at a time, beating well between additions.
• Purée the bananas with the curdled milk and vanilla.
• Beat the dry ingredients and the banana mixture alternately into the butter mixture at medium speed in two additions.
• Scrape the batter into the prepared pan and bake for 1 hour, until a wooden toothpick comes out clean.
• Cool and top with fudge frosting.

Fudge Frosting

- ½ cup sugar
- 2 tbs corn syrup
- ¼ cup cocoa powder
- 3 tbs butter
- 2 cups confectioners' sugar

• Warm the sugar with ¼ cup water and the corn syrup and heat for a couple of minutes until the sugar has melted. Stir in the cocoa powder then add the butter.
• Remove from the heat and stir well.
• Transfer to a large mixing bowl and beat in the confectioners' sugar together with 2 tablespoons of hot water.
• Use to frost the banana cake.

Drunken Christmas Fruitcake Cookies

These are delightful cookies that will be a crowd pleaser.

- 1 cup candied cherries
- 1 cup seedless raisins
- 1 cup seedless currants
- ½ cup candied citron peel
- 3 cups mixed nuts, such as pecans, walnuts and almonds
- ¼ cup butter
- ½ cup brown sugar
- 2 eggs
- 2 tbs milk
- ¼ cup sherry, rum or grape juice
- 1½ cups all-purpose flour
- 1½ tsp baking soda
- ½ tsp allspice powder
- ½ tsp ground cloves
- ½ tsp grated nutmeg

- Preheat oven to 250°F.
- Chop the fruit and nuts in a food processor until fine and set aside.
- Cream the butter and sugar in a medium bowl until fluffy. Stir in the eggs, milk and liquor or grape juice.
- Sift the flour with the baking soda, allspice, cloves and nutmeg. Add half of this to the creamed mixture and mix well. Blend the other half with the chopped fruit and nuts, then combine both batters together.
- Drop the mixture in 2-tablespoon size mounds onto a baking sheet and flatten the top of each cookie with the back of a spoon.
- Bake for 30–35 minutes until cooked.

Makes 36

Fruit & Chocolate Chews

A little bit of this, a little bit of that – these cookies seem to have all the ingredients of the festive season!

- ½ cup raisins
- ½ cup chopped candied cherries
- ¼ cup cherry brandy
- ¾ cup unsalted butter
- ½ cup granulated sugar
- ¾ cup brown sugar
- 1 egg
- 1 tsp vanilla extract
- 2½ cups all-purpose flour
- 1 tsp baking soda
- ¼ tsp salt
- ½ cup chocolate chips
- ½ cup chopped walnuts

- Preheat oven to 350°F.
- Soak the raisins and cherries in the cherry brandy.
- Using an electric mixer, cream the butter with the sugars in a large bowl until light and fluffy. Add the egg and vanilla and beat well.
- Combine the flour, baking soda and salt in a small bowl.
- Add the flour mixture gradually to the butter mixture and beat just until blended.
- Stir in the raisins, cherries, chocolate chips and walnuts by hand, just until combined.
- Drop teaspoonfuls of the cookie dough onto lined baking sheets.
- Bake for 10–15 minutes until light and almost set.
- Cool on wire racks.

Makes about 36

Cornmeal Coconut Cake

This combination of cornmeal and coconut makes a delicious cake, just right to be served at tea time.

- **1 cup butter**
- **1 cup sugar**
- **2 eggs**
- **1 cup all-purpose flour**
- **1 cup cornmeal**
- **2 tsp baking powder**
- **1 tsp ground cinnamon**
- **½ tsp grated nutmeg**
- **1 cup grated fresh coconut**
- **1 cup milk**
- **1 tsp vanilla extract**

- Preheat oven to 350°F. Line, grease and flour a 9 inch cake pan.
- Cream the butter with the sugar in the bowl of an electric mixer until light and fluffy. Add the eggs one at a time.
- Sift the flour and add the cornmeal, baking powder, spices and coconut.
- Combine the milk with the vanilla.
- Add the flour mixture and milk alternately to the creamed mixture in three additions, beginning and ending with flour.
- Turn into the prepared pan and bake for 35–40 minutes, until a wooden toothpick inserted into the center comes out clean and the cake begins to shrink from the sides of the pan.
- Remove and cool for 5 minutes before turning out.

Warm Cinnamon Walnut Sponge with Orange-scented Rum Syrup

- **2 cups chopped walnuts**
- **4 eggs**
- **2 cups granulated sugar**
- **1 tsp vanilla extract**
- **3 cups all-purpose flour**
- **4 tsp baking powder**
- **1 tsp ground cinnamon**
- **1 cup warm milk**
- **¼ cup melted butter**
- **heavy cream to serve**

• Preheat oven to 350ºF. Grease and flour a 10 inch tube pan.
• Sprinkle the nuts onto the bottom of the pan and set aside.
• Beat the eggs with the sugar and vanilla until light and fluffy and doubled in volume, about 4 minutes.
• Sift the flour with the baking powder and cinnamon. Fold in the flour and beat for a further 2 minutes.
• Add the milk to the butter. Add to the batter and beat for about 1 minute more until the mixture is creamy.
• Pour the batter into the prepared tin and bake for 50–60 minutes until well risen, golden and the cake begins to pull away from the tin.
• Remove from oven and run a knife around the cake to loosen it from the edges.
• Wait 5 minutes then turn the cake out of the pan. Using a long wooden skewer, make holes right through the cake.
• Spoon the warm glaze onto the cake until it is all used up and the cake is soaked with the syrup.
• Serve the cake with a dollop of heavy cream.

Serves 10

Orange-scented Rum Syrup

- **½ cup unsalted butter**
- **1 cup granulated sugar**
- **1 tbs orange zest**
- **½ tsp grated nutmeg**
- **⅔ cup dark or golden rum**
- **½ tsp aromatic bitters**

• Melt the butter in a small saucepan. Add the sugar and ¼ cup water and stir to dissolve the sugar. Add the orange zest and nutmeg. Boil for about 3–5 minutes, then remove and add the rum and bitters.
• Spoon onto the cake as in the directions above.

Coconut Chiffon Cake

A tropical twist on a traditional recipe, frost this with a fluffy white frosting.

- 2¼ cups sifted cake flour
- 1 tbs baking powder
- ½ tsp ground cinnamon
- ½ tsp salt
- 5 eggs, separated, plus 1 whole egg
- 1⅓ cups granulated sugar
- ½ cup vegetable oil
- ⅔ cup orange juice
- ¼ tsp cream of tartar
- 1 cup freshly grated coconut

- Preheat oven to 325ºF.
- Combine the flour, baking powder, cinnamon and salt. Sift three times.
- Place the egg yolks and whole egg into a bowl and beat with an electric beater until frothy. Gradually add 1 cup sugar, and beat until thick, fluffy and light in color, about 5 minutes.
- Slowly pour in the oil in a steady stream and continue beating for about 1 minute longer.
- Add the dry ingredients to the yolk mixture alternately with the orange juice in three additions, beginning and ending with flour.
- Wash and dry the beaters and beat the egg whites with the cream of tartar until frothy. Gradually add the remaining sugar and beat to a soft meringue.
- With a large spatula fold a quarter of the yolk mixture into the whites and then fold the whites into the yolk mixture in four additions, taking care not to over fold.

- Gently pour or spoon the batter into a 10 inch ungreased Bundt pan.
- Bake for 60–65 minutes until springy to touch. Invert the cake and cool completely in the pan before removing.
- Frost the cake with fluffy white frosting and sprinkle with the grated coconut.

Serves 10

Fluffy White Frosting

- 1½ cups granulated sugar
- 1 tbs corn syrup
- 2 egg whites
- ½ tsp cream of tartar

- Place the sugar, corn syrup and ⅓ cup water into a saucepan and boil until the thread stage is reached.
- Beat the egg whites until fluffy, add the cream of tartar, pour in the sugar solution and beat continuously until the mixture begins to lose its sheen somewhat.

White Coconut Cake

- **1 cup milk**
- **1½ cups freshly grated coconut**
- **2½ cups cake flour**
- **1 tbs baking powder**
- **½ tsp salt**
- **½ cup butter**
- **1½ cups granulated sugar**
- **5 egg whites**
- **1 tsp vanilla extract**
- **fluffy white frosting (opposite)**

• Preheat oven to 350ºF. Line, grease and flour two 9 inch round cake pans.

• Bring the milk to a boil, add ½ cup coconut, remove from the heat and let steep for 30 minutes. Purée and set aside.

• Combine the flour, baking powder and salt.

• Cream the butter with the sugar until light and fluffy. Add the unbeaten egg whites and continue to beat until creamy; the mixture will not become very fluffy, but it should be thick and creamy. Add the vanilla.

• Add the flour and coconut milk mixture alternately to the creamed mixture in three additions, beginning and ending with the flour.

• Divide the batter equally among the prepared cake pans.

• Bake in the middle of the oven until golden, about 30 minutes.

• Cool in the pans for 5 minutes then turn out onto cooling racks.

• To finish the cake: place one layer upside down on a plate, spread about ¼ cup frosting onto this layer, sprinkle with some of the remaining coconut, then place the second layer on top. Frost the top and sides of the cake and decorate with the balance of the grated coconut.

Serves 8–10

Cinnamon & Currant Stuffed Pastry Roll

- **2 cups good quality seedless currants, washed and dried**
- **1 tsp ground cinnamon**
- **¼ cup granulated sugar**
- **2 tbs melted butter**
- **1 cup bread crumbs**
- **egg white for brushing**

FOR THE PASTRY
- **2 cups all-purpose flour**
- **6 tbs shortening**
- **4 tbs unsalted butter**
- **1 tbs vinegar**

- To make the pastry: place the flour in a large bowl. Cut the shortening into the flour until it disappears.
- Cut the butter into ½ inch cubes and toss with the flour mixture but do not incorporate.
- Combine the vinegar with ⅓ cup cold water. Sprinkle the liquid evenly over the flour mixture and gather together loosely. It will be very rough.
- Turn the dough out onto a floured surface and pat into a rough rectangle. Roll into a rectangle about 10 x 16 inches.
- Fold the long ends of dough into the center and then fold in half like a book. With the smooth end on your left, roll into another rectangle and fold again in the same way. Turn dough as before and roll and fold a third time. Refrigerate dough for about 30 minutes. Wrap until ready for use.
- Preheat oven to 375ºF.
- Combine the currants with the cinnamon and sugar.
- Roll the pastry into a ¼ inch thick rectangle, approximately 12 X 20 inches, and brush with the melted butter.
- Sprinkle with the bread crumbs, then sprinkle the currant mixture evenly on top.
- Beginning at a long end, roll up jellyroll style, seal the ends and place on a baking tray, seam side down. Brush with egg white and sprinkle with sugar.
- Bake for 45–50 minutes until golden.
- Remove from the oven and cool slightly, then slice the log diagonally into pieces about 1½ inches in width. Place these back on the baking tray and return to the oven for a further 10 minutes.
- Remove and cool on racks.

Makes 10–12

Carrot Coconut Loaf

- **3 cups all-purpose flour**
- **1½ tsp baking powder**
- **1½ tsp baking soda**
- **2 tsp ground cinnamon**
- **½ tsp grated nutmeg**
- **4 large eggs**
- **2 cups brown sugar**
- **½ cup vegetable oil**
- **1 cup finely grated coconut**
- **1 tsp vanilla extract**
- **1½ cups grated carrots**
- **1 cup orange juice**
- **2 tsp grated orange zest**

- Preheat oven to 375ºF.
- Combine the flour, baking powder, baking soda, cinnamon and nutmeg in a large bowl.
- In a separate bowl, beat the eggs with the sugar until thick. Add the oil, coconut, vanilla, carrots, orange juice and zest.
- Pour the wet mixture into the dry ingredients and stir to combine.
- Spoon the mixture into 2 greased loaf pans and bake for 45 minutes until a wooden toothpick inserted into the center comes out clean.

Makes 2

Coconut Oatmeal Cookies

- **½ cup butter**
- **1¼ cups brown sugar**
- **1 egg**
- **½ cup whole wheat flour**
- **½ cup all-purpose flour**
- **1 cup rolled oats**
- **½ cup finely grated coconut**
- **1 tsp baking powder**
- **¼ tsp baking soda**
- **½ cup currants or raisins**

- Preheat oven to 350ºF.
- Combine the butter with the sugar and beat until light and fluffy. Add the egg and beat until combined.
- Combine the flours, oats, coconut, baking powder and soda. Add to the egg mixture and fold in the currants or raisins.
- Drop teaspoonfuls onto a greased baking sheet and lightly press to flatten. Bake for 12 minutes for soft chewy cookies or 15 minutes for crisper cookies.

Makes 36

Grenada Spice Cake with Caramel Rum Glaze

Grenada is renowned for its spice markets, especially its nutmeg, and this cake showcases the flavors well.

- ½ cup unsalted butter
- 1 cup brown sugar
- 2 eggs
- 1 tsp vanilla extract
- 2⅓ cups cake flour
- 2 tsp baking powder
- ½ tsp baking soda
- 1 tsp ground cinnamon
- ¼ tsp ground cloves
- ½ tsp grated nutmeg
- ¼ tsp allspice powder
- 1 cup plain yogurt
- 1 cup toasted pecans, finely chopped, plus extra to decorate

• Preheat oven to 350ºF. Grease and flour an 8 inch ring cake pan.
• Cream the butter with the sugar until light and creamy. Add the eggs one at a time, beating well between additions. Add the vanilla.
• Sift together the flour, baking powder, baking soda and dried spices.
• Add the dry ingredients to the creamed mixture alternately with the yogurt, in three additions, beginning and ending with flour.
• Fold in the nuts; the batter will be quite stiff.
• Spoon into the prepared pan and bake for 50 minutes until a wooden toothpick comes out clean.

• Invert the cake and leave for 5 minutes in pan, then remove, place cake right-side up and pour on the caramel glaze, letting it run down the sides. Decorate with toasted pecans.

Serves 8–10

Caramel Rum Glaze

- 4 tbs butter
- 4 tbs brown sugar
- ¼ cup evaporated milk
- 2 tbs rum
- ¾–1 cup sifted confectioners' sugar
- 1 tsp vanilla extract

• Melt the butter in a small heavy saucepan, add the brown sugar and cook, stirring, until the sugar has melted. Add the evaporated milk, remove from heat, stir well, and add the rum. Place back on heat and cook until creamy.
• Remove from heat and beat in the confectioners' sugar until the mixture is of a pourable consistency. Add the vanilla and stir.
• Pour the glaze onto the cake.

Nutmeg Muffins

- **2 cups all-purpose flour**
- **¾ cup brown sugar**
- **1 tbs baking powder**
- **2 tsp grated nutmeg**
- **pinch of salt**
- **1 egg**
- **¾ cup milk**
- **⅓ cup vegetable oil**
- **1 tsp vanilla extract**

- Preheat oven to 350ºF.
- Combine all the dry ingredients in a mixing bowl.
- Beat the egg with the milk and add the oil and vanilla.
- Add to the dry ingredients and stir just to combine.
- Spoon into greased muffin pans and bake for 20–25 minutes until risen and golden.

Makes 10

Coconut Scones

- **2 cups all-purpose flour**
- **1 tbs baking powder**
- **½ cup granulated sugar**
- **½ tsp ground cinnamon**
- **⅛ tsp ground cloves**
- **½ cup finely grated fresh coconut**
- **¼ cup softened butter**
- **1 cup milk**
- **1 egg**

- Preheat oven to 375ºF.
- Combine all the dry ingredients, add the coconut and mix. Add the butter and rub into the mixture until it is crumbly.
- Combine the milk with the egg, add to the flour mixture and stir to a sticky dough.
- Turn onto a floured surface and divide into 2 rounds. Pat out each round to ¾ inch thickness and cut into 6 triangles.
- Place on a baking sheet, brush with a little milk and sprinkle with sugar.
- Bake for 15–20 minutes until risen and golden.

Makes 12

Cinnamon & Brown Sugar Swirl Buns

- **1 tbs instant yeast**
- **1 cup lukewarm milk**
- **⅓ cup sugar**
- **⅓ cup butter, melted**
- **1 tsp salt**
- **1 tsp cinnamon**
- **¼ tsp ground cloves**
- **½ tsp grated nutmeg**
- **2 eggs**
- **4–4½ cups all-purpose flour**

FOR THE FILLING
- **½ cup butter, melted**
- **1 cup brown sugar**
- **1 tsp ground cinnamon**
- **2 cups raisins**

- In a large bowl, dissolve the yeast in ¼ cup warm water and stir in the milk, sugar, butter, salt, cinnamon, cloves, nutmeg, eggs and 2 cups flour. Beat until smooth, adding enough flour to make the dough easy to handle.
- Turn the dough onto a lightly floured surface and knead until smooth and elastic, about 5 minutes.
- Place in a greased bowl, then turn greased side up. Cover and let rise until doubled in bulk, about 1½ hours.

- Punch down dough and divide in half. Roll each half into a 12 x 8 inch rectangle.
- Spread each rectangle with the melted butter and sprinkle with the sugar and cinnamon, followed by the raisins. Roll up jellyroll style and cut into 1½ inch pieces.
- Place on a greased baking sheet and let the buns rise until doubled in size, about 20–30 minutes.
- Preheat oven to 375°F.
- Bake until golden brown, about 20 minutes.
- Frost the buns with powdered sugar frosting.

Makes 20–24

Powdered Sugar Frosting

- **1 cup confectioners' sugar**
- **1 tbs orange juice**
- **½ tsp vanilla extract**

- Combine all the ingredients.

Carrot Pineapple Muffins

- **8 oz can crushed pineapple**
- **milk (see method)**
- **2 cups all-purpose flour**
- **⅓ cup brown sugar**
- **1 tbs baking powder**
- **2 eggs**
- **⅓ cup vegetable oil**
- **¾ cup grated carrot**
  (about 1 large carrot)
- **1 tsp vanilla extract**
- **2 tbs granulated sugar**
- **½ tsp ground cinnamon**

- Preheat oven to 375ºF.
- Drain the pineapple, reserving syrup; add enough milk to the syrup to measure ¾ cup.
- Stir together the flour, brown sugar, baking powder and some salt in a mixing bowl.
- In another bowl, beat the eggs until fluffy. Add the milk mixture, oil, carrots, vanilla and drained pineapple.
- Add the wet mixture to the flour mixture and stir just until combined.
- Spoon into greased muffin cups.
- Combine the granulated sugar with the cinnamon. Sprinkle onto the muffins and bake for 20–25 minutes.

Makes 12

Cinnamon Crisps

- **3½–4 cups all-purpose flour**
- **1 tbs instant yeast**
- **¼ cup granulated sugar**
- **1 tsp salt**
- **¼ cup butter**
- **1¼ cups milk**
- **1 egg**

FOR THE FILLING
- **½ cup brown sugar**
- **½ cup granulated sugar**
- **1 tsp ground cinnamon**
- **¼ cup melted butter**

FOR THE TOPPING
- **½ cup chopped nuts**
  (almonds, pecans, walnuts)
- **1 tsp ground cinnamon**
- **1 cup granulated sugar**
- **¼ cup melted butter**

• Prepare the dough. Combine 2 cups flour, the yeast, sugar and salt. Melt the butter with the milk to a temperature of about 115–120ºF. Add to the flour with the egg and mix to a soft dough, adding as much of the remaining flour as is necessary to make a soft and pliable dough. Cover and let rise until doubled in volume, about 45 minutes.
• Punch dough down and divide in half.

• To make the filling: combine all the filling ingredients except the melted butter.
• Roll each piece of dough into a 12 inch square. Brush each square with the melted butter; sprinkle with the cinnamon sugar mixture. Roll up jellyroll style, beginning at the longest side, seal seams and cut each into 12 rolls.
• Place the rolls onto a greased or lined baking sheet and flatten to about 3 inches in diameter.
• Cover and let rest for about 20 minutes.
• Preheat oven to 400ºF.
• Cover the rolls with waxed paper and, using a rolling pin, flatten to ⅛ inch thickness. Remove the paper.
• Meanwhile, make the topping: combine all the topping ingredients except the melted butter.
• Brush the flattened rolls with the melted butter, sprinkle with the topping and cover with waxed paper.
• Bake for 10–12 minutes.

Makes 24

Plantain Tarts

This is a Jamaican tart made from ripe plantains
infused with local spices.

- **2½ cups all-purpose flour**
- **1 tsp salt**
- **½ cup unsalted cold butter**
- **½ cup shortening**
- **½ cup iced water**

FOR THE FILLING
- **¼ cup sugar**
- **1 ripe plantain, peeled and chopped**
- **½ tsp grated nutmeg**

• Prepare the pastry. Place the
flour and salt in the bowl of a
food processor. Cut the butter and
shortening into small pieces and
drop onto the flour. Pulse in the food
processor until the mixture resembles
fine crumbs.

• Add some of the water and pulse
a few times. Add more water and
pulse again. Continue until the
mixture has curds, and clumps
and sticks together when pressed
between your fingers.
• Remove and form into a ball.
Wrap and chill for at least 2 hours.
• To make the filling: bring ¼ cup
water to a boil with the sugar.
Add the plantain and simmer until
tender, about 10–15 minutes.
• Mash the plantain and add the
nutmeg. Leave the mixture to cool.
• Preheat oven to 400°F.
• Divide the dough in half and roll
out each piece to ⅛ inch thickness.
Cut into 4 inch rounds.
• Spoon the cooled filling onto the
center of the lower half of each
round. Fold over and seal with the
prongs of a fork.
• Place on a baking sheet and bake
for 20 minutes until golden.

Makes about 16

PLANTAINS

Tipsy Fruit-filled Ladder Loaf

Soaking the fruits in rum ahead of time gives them
a chance to absorb all that flavor,
which is released later on during baking!

- 2 cups flour
- 4 tsp baking powder
- ½ cup butter
- 2 oz cream cheese
- ¼ cup milk
- ½ cup brown sugar
- ½ tsp ground cinnamon
- 1 cup dried fruit, soaked in ¼ cup rum for 1 hour

- Combine the flour and baking powder and rub in the butter followed by the cream cheese until the mixture resembles fine crumbs.
- Add the milk and gently knead.
- Refrigerate to let the pastry firm up.
- Preheat oven to 425ºF.
- Roll out the pastry to a 12 x 8 inch rectangle. Transfer to a baking sheet.
- Sprinkle the brown sugar and cinnamon onto the center third of the pastry. Cover with the fruit.
- Cut 2½ inch slats along the two outside edges and bring the strips together. Pinch to seal.
- Bake for 15 minutes.
- Drizzle with powdered sugar frosting (page 284) if wished.

Cornmeal Bake
with Roasted Red Peppers
& Chives

- **2 cups cornmeal**
- **2 cups boiling water**
- **2 cups all-purpose flour**
- **1 tsp salt**
- **3 tsp instant yeast**
- **¼ cup brown sugar**
- **⅓ cup softened butter**
- **1 cup warm water (110–120ºF)**
- **1 roasted red pepper, chopped**
- **⅓ cup chopped chives**

• Combine the cornmeal with the boiling water and stir well. Place into the bowl of an electric mixer or food processor and add the flour, salt, yeast and sugar. Mix, then add the softened butter and combine with the flour until crumbly in texture. Add the water and knead to a soft dough.
• Add the roasted pepper and chives and continue kneading.
• Let rest until doubled in volume, about 30 minutes.
• Preheat oven to 400ºF.
• Roll the dough into two 8 inch circles about 2 inches thick.
• Prick the bakes with a fork and leave for a further 20 minutes.
• Place on a baking sheet and bake for 30–40 minutes.

Makes 2

Whole Wheat Island Pizza Twists

- **1 tbs olive oil**
- **½ cup Italian tomato sauce (page 137)**
- **½ cup grated Parmesan cheese**
- **1 tsp dried Italian herbs, such as oregano**

FOR THE DOUGH
- **¾ cup milk**
- **1½ cups bread flour**
- **½ cup whole wheat flour**
- **2 tsp instant yeast**
- **1 tbs sugar**
- **1 tsp salt**
- **1 cup finely chopped Spanish thyme (or any fresh thyme)**
- **1 tsp minced garlic**
- **2 tbs melted shortening**

- To make the dough: heat the milk to 115ºF.
- Place the flours, yeast, sugar, salt, thyme and garlic into a mixing bowl. Add the shortening and milk and knead to a soft smooth dough.
- Cover and let rise until doubled in size, about 60 minutes.
- Punch down the dough. Let rest for 10 minutes.
- Preheat oven to 400ºF.
- Roll out the dough to a rectangle about ½ inch thick. Brush with the oil, spread the tomato sauce over thinly and sprinkle with the cheese, herbs, salt and freshly ground black pepper.
- Cut into pieces, 8 inches long and 1 inch wide, and twist each length.
- Place onto a baking tray. Bake for 15 minutes until lightly browned.

Makes about 18

Savory Drop Scones

**These scones are a great accompaniment
to any meal or are good as a snack as well.**

- ¾ cup milk
- 1 tablespoon fresh lime juice
- 2 cups all-purpose flour
- 2 tsp baking powder
- ¼ tsp baking soda
- 1 tsp salt
- 1 tsp coarsely ground black pepper
- ½ cup grated Parmesan cheese
- 3 tbs butter
- 3 tbs shortening
- 1 egg
- ⅓ cup chopped chives
- 2 pimento peppers, seeded
  and chopped

- Preheat oven to 375ºF.
- Mix the milk and lime juice and let stand for 10 minutes until curdled.
- Combine the flour, baking powder, baking soda, salt, black pepper and cheese.
- Add the butter and shortening and rub into the flour until the mixture resembles small peas.
- Combine the egg with the milk and add to the flour mixture. Add the chives and pimentos and stir gently. The batter should be soft.
- Drop tablespoonfuls onto a greased baking sheet. Sprinkle with additional Parmesan cheese if desired.
- Bake for 15–20 minutes until risen and golden.

Makes 12

Cornmeal Biscuits
with Cilantro & Chili

- **1½ cups flour**
- **½ cup cornmeal**
- **1 tbs chili powder**
- **4 tsp baking powder**
- **½ tsp salt**
- **2 tsp sugar**
- **½ cup shortening**
- **⅔ cup milk**
- **¼ cup chopped cilantro (chadon beni) (optional)**

- Preheat oven to 450ºF.
- Combine all the dry ingredients in a mixing bowl.
- Rub shortening into the mixture until it resembles peas. Add the milk and cilantro.
- Bring the mixture together with your hands and divide into two.
- Press each half out to ¾ inch thickness and stamp out with a 2½ inch cutter.
- Place on a greased baking sheet and bake for 10–12 minutes until risen and golden.

Makes 10–12

Sundried Tomato Flatbread

- **2½ cups sifted all-purpose flour**
- **½ tbs instant yeast**
- **½ tsp salt**
- **2½ tbs olive oil**
- **1 cup warm water (105–115ºF)**
- **⅓ cup diced sundried tomatoes**

FOR THE TOPPING
- **1 tsp dried oregano**
- **1 tsp sea salt**
- **2 tbs olive oil plus extra for brushing**
- **cilantro (chadon beni)**

- In a small bowl combine the flour with the yeast and salt.
- Mix the olive oil with the water. Add to the flour mixture and combine; the dough should be soft and sticky. Add the sundried tomatoes and knead lightly.
- Shape the dough into a ball and place in a greased bowl. It doesn't matter if the dough feels sticky at this point. Cover with plastic wrap and let stand until doubled in bulk, about 45–60 minutes.
- Grease a 15 x 10 x 1 inch baking sheet with olive oil.
- Punch down the dough with your fist, place on the baking sheet and pat it out to the edges with your hands. You can use a rolling pin if you find this easier. Drizzle on the 2 tablespoons of olive oil and sprinkle with the salt and oregano.
- Cover and let rise for about 30 minutes. Meanwhile, preheat oven to 400ºF.
- Bake for 20 minutes until crisp and browned.
- Brush with olive oil and sprinkle with cilantro.
- Cool and cut into squares.

Makes 15

West Indian Bakery Bread

- **5–6 cups flour**
- **1 package instant yeast**
- **2 tsp salt**
- **1 tbs sugar**
- **2½ cups warm milk (105–120°F)**
- **½ cup butter or shortening or mixed, melted**
- **2 eggs**

• Place 2 cups flour, the yeast, salt and sugar in the bowl of an electric mixer.
• Add the milk, melted fat and eggs and beat until smooth.
• Add the rest of the flour and knead to a soft smooth dough, about 5 minutes.
• Cover and let rise until doubled in volume, about 45–60 minutes.
• Punch down the dough and divide in half.
• Grease 2 loaf pans.
• Roll each piece of dough into a 10 inch rectangle. Roll up each one and place seam side down into a loaf pan. Cover and let rise until doubled in volume, about 45 minutes.
• Preheat oven to 400°F.
• Bake for 25–30 minutes until the bottoms of the loaves sound hollow when tapped.

Makes 2

Dinner Rolls

• Divide each piece of dough into 8 pieces. Form into smooth balls. Cover and let rise for 30 minutes.
• Bake for 20 minutes until golden.

Makes 16

Dosti Roti

**A layered roti that's very similar to paratha.
Serve with any curried dishes.**

- **4 cups all-purpose flour**
- **1 tbs butter, softened**
- **1 tsp salt**
- **4 tsp baking powder**
- **½ cup ghee**

- Combine the flour with the butter, salt and baking powder.
- Add enough water to knead to a soft dough, cover and rest for 30 minutes.
- Divide the dough into 8 pieces. Form each piece into a ball. Let rest for 15 minutes.
- Divide each ball (loya) into two and flatten slightly. Paste some ghee onto half the pieces, then cover with another flattened loya, like a sandwich. Press together, cover and let rest for 30 minutes.
- Melt the remaining ghee.
- Lightly flour a surface, roll each piece of prepared dough into an 8–10 inch circle and cook on a hot baking stone. Turn, brush with ghee, turn again and brush with ghee.
- Cook until it balloons, then remove.
- Split the dosti into two and wrap in a tea towel. Repeat with the remaining circles of dough.

Garlic Crescents

- **3–4 cups all-purpose flour**
- **¼ cup sugar**
- **1 tsp salt**
- **2 tbs instant yeast**
- **2 cups milk**
- **½ cup butter, melted**
- **1 egg white, beaten**
- **1 tbs poppy seeds**

FOR THE FILLING
- **½ cup softened butter**
- **1 tbs minced garlic**
- **½ tsp salt**

• Prepare the dough. In a large bowl combine 2 cups all-purpose flour with the sugar, salt and yeast.
• Warm the milk to 115–120ºF, add the melted butter and combine.
• Add the milk mixture to the flour mixture and knead to a soft dough, adding as much of the remaining flour as you can to make a soft but pliable dough. Cover and let rise until doubled in volume, about 60 minutes.
• Divide the dough into 3 equal portions and form each portion into a ball. Cover and let rest for 10 minutes.

• To make the filling: combine the butter, garlic and salt.
• On a lightly floured surface roll one ball of dough into a 12 inch circle, spread with 2 tablespoons of the filling, more if necessary but don't cover the dough too thickly with butter.
• Cut the circle into 12 wedges. To shape the rolls begin at the wide end of the wedge and roll towards the point. Place the rolls point down, 2–3 inches apart, on a greased baking sheet.
• Brush with beaten egg white and sprinkle with poppy seeds. Repeat for the other 2 rounds.
• Cover and let rise until doubled in volume, about 20 minutes.
• Preheat oven to 400ºF.
• Bake the crescents for 12–15 minutes until nicely browned.

Makes 36

Cheese Braid

- 2½–3 cups all-purpose flour
- 1 tbs sugar
- 1 tsp salt
- 1 tbs instant yeast
- 2 cups grated cheese
- 1 cup milk
- ¼ cup butter, melted
- 1 egg, beaten

• Prepare the dough. In a large bowl combine the flour, sugar, salt and yeast. Add 1 cup cheese.

• Warm the milk to 115–120ºF, add the melted butter and combine. Add the beaten egg.

• Add the milk mixture to the flour mixture and knead to a soft dough, adding as much of the remaining flour as you can to form a soft but pliable dough. Cover and let rise until doubled in volume, about 45 minutes.

• Roll out the dough to an 8 x 16 inch rectangle. Divide into 3 equal sections. Pinch the dough together at the top, then make the braid by bringing the left section over the middle followed by the right section. Continue the braid down to the end and tuck the last piece under.

• Sprinkle with the remaining cheese. Cover and let rise until doubled in volume, about 20 minutes.

• Preheat oven to 400ºF.

• Bake for 20–25 minutes until nicely browned.

Multigrain Bread

- **2½ cups milk**
- **¼ cup vegetable oil or melted butter**
- **2 packages instant yeast**
- **⅓ cup brown sugar**
- **½ cup cornmeal**
- **⅓ cup wheat bran**
- **¾ cup whole wheat flour**
- **1 cup rolled oats**
- **4–5 cups bread flour**
- **2 tsp salt**

• Heat the milk to 105–115°F. Combine with the vegetable oil or melted butter.

• In a large mixing bowl combine the yeast, sugar, cornmeal, wheat bran, whole wheat flour, oats and 2 cups bread flour. Add the salt and stir to combine.

• Add the liquid and stir. Knead in as much of the rest of the flour as is necessary to make a soft springy dough.

• Do not let the dough get too dry. Place in a covered bowl and let rise until doubled in volume, about 1 hour.

• Punch down dough and divide in half. Form into loaves and place into greased loaf pans. Cover and let rise for another 45–50 minutes.

• Preheat oven to 400°F.

• Bake for about 35 minutes or until the loaves are browned and sound hollow when the bottoms are tapped.

Makes 2

Plantain Bread

A savory Spanish Caribbean bread, this tastes a little like banana bread, though the plantains give a milder flavor, and the addition of herbs makes it a wonderful dinner bread!

- 2 cups all-purpose flour
- 1 tsp baking soda
- 1 tsp salt
- pinch of grated nutmeg
- ½ cup chopped chives
- 2 eggs
- ¼ cup sour cream (or ¼ cup milk combined with 1 tsp vinegar)
- 1 cup mashed ripe plantain
- 1 tsp freshly ground black pepper
- ⅓ cup grated Parmesan cheese

- Preheat oven to 375ºF.
- Place the flour, baking soda, salt, nutmeg and chives in a mixing bowl.
- Beat the eggs and combine with the sour cream and plantain.
- Add to the dry mixture and stir just to combine.
- Place the mixture into a 9 inch square baking pan. Sprinkle with the black pepper and cheese.
- Bake for 30 minutes until risen and golden.

Serves 6–8

Stuffed Paratha Roti

This is a delightful variation of the regular paratha and will
go well with any East Indian dish.

- **4 cups flour**
- **1 tbs butter, softened, plus
  2 tbs melted butter**
- **1 tsp salt**
- **4 tsp baking powder**
- **2 tbs vegetable oil**

FOR THE FILLING
- **4 tbs butter, softened**
- **½ tsp garam masala (see page 151)**
- **1 tsp ground roasted cumin (geera)**
- **1 tbs minced ginger**
- **1 tbs minced garlic**

• Make the dough. Combine the
flour with the butter, salt and baking
powder. Add enough water to knead
to a very soft dough. Cover and rest
for 45 minutes.
• Divide the dough into 8 pieces
and form each piece into a ball.
• Combine the melted butter
with the oil.

• To make the filling: combine the
filling ingredients and set aside.
• Roll out each piece of dough into
a 6 inch round. Place about ¾
tablespoon of the filling mixture onto
the dough and spread to the ends.
• Cut the dough into half from
the middle of the top edge; leave a
1 inch uncut portion at the base.
Starting from the top right hand side
portion, roll the dough all the way
to the bottom and up the left side.
Your dough should resemble a cone.
Tuck the end under and then push
the pointed part into the dough and
flatten slightly. Rest for a further
30 minutes.
• On a lightly floured surface roll
each piece of prepared dough into
an 8 inch circle.
• Cook on a hot baking stone.
Turn, brush with the oil mixture, turn
again and brush with oil. Cook until it
balloons, then remove.
• Beat the roti with your hands or a
wooden spatula to break and flake.

Makes 8

condiments

Hot sauces or peppers form part of the foundation of Caribbean cookery, and so you are certain to find pepper sauce of some type in a West Indian or Caribbean home. Here, pepper sauces stand alongside all other condiments in restaurants; they are packed in plastic pouches and go out with fast food orders along with mustard and ketchup. Sometimes when your meal needs a little 'pick me up' or you're about to enjoy that rice and meat cookup, or curry meal, a few drops of pepper sauce will give you that perfect flavor every time! Many homes have pepper trees in their back yards and, if not, hot peppers are available in our markets seven days a week! It's not unusual to see bottles of homemade pepper sauces standing out on ledges or tables in people's back yards – the sunshine, they claim, makes the pepper sauce 'cure' or taste hotter!

Other condiments include fruit chutneys to accompany Indian-inspired fritters or grilled meats, Mexican salsas and West Indian pestos, all infused with our very own habaneros or scotch bonnets.

Papaya & Apple Chutney

- **1 cup white vinegar**
- **1 cup brown sugar**
- **2 cups chopped papaya**
- **2 cups chopped apples**
- **¼ tsp allspice powder**
- **¼ tsp whole cloves**
- **1 tsp ground cinnamon**
- **1 onion, chopped**
- **1 hot pepper**
- **½ tsp salt**

- Put the vinegar in a saucepan and bring to a boil. Add the sugar, stir, then add all the other ingredients. Stir, then cook slowly on a low heat for 30 minutes until tender and thick.
- Remove the hot pepper, and spoon into sterilized jars.
- Serve with grilled meats and fish.

Makes two 14 oz jars

Tamarind Chutney

- **2 cups peeled, ripe tamarind pods**
- **2 tbs salt**
- **2 cups granulated sugar**
- **2 tbs freshly ground roasted cumin (geera)**
- **½ hot pepper, seeded and minced (more or less to taste)**
- **6 garlic cloves, minced**

- Put the tamarind pods in a small saucepan and barely cover with boiling water. Let steep for 30 minutes or boil for 5 minutes.
- Remove the seeds from the tamarind and discard (a potato crusher works well to separate the seeds from the pulp).
- Add the salt, sugar, cumin, pepper and garlic to the tamarind and stir to mix.
- Bring the mixture to a boil and remove from heat.
- Cool, taste and adjust seasonings. The chutney should be slightly sour–sweet in taste.

Makes 1 cup

Spicy Tomato Salsa

- **6 large, ripe tomatoes, peeled**
- **1 tsp minced garlic**
- **1 tbs olive oil**
- **1 tbs fresh lime juice**
- **½ habanero or scotch bonnet pepper, seeded and chopped**
- **½ cup finely chopped chives**
- **1 tsp chili powder**
- **2 tbs finely chopped cilantro (chadon beni)**

- Chop the tomatoes, and combine with the garlic, olive oil, lime juice, pepper, chives, chili powder, and salt and freshly ground black pepper. Taste and adjust seasonings.
- Before serving, add cilantro and stir.
- Serve with corn chips, grilled chicken or fish, or with your favorite Mexican dish.

Makes about 2 cups

Chadon Beni Pesto

- **10 chadon beni (cilantro) leaves**
- **2 large Spanish thyme leaves**
- **juice of 1 large lime**
- **6 garlic cloves**
- **salt to taste**
- **1 hot pepper, seeded and chopped**
- **½ cup olive oil**

- Put all the ingredients except the oil in a blender and purée.
- Gradually add the oil to make a thick emulsion.
- Serve with grilled fish or meats, or drizzle on top of fish sandwiches.

Makes about ¾ cup

Green Mango & Thyme Chutney

- 4 green mangoes
- 2 garlic cloves, minced
- 2 Spanish thyme leaves
- ¼ cup chopped cilantro (chadon beni)
- salt to taste
- 1 hot pepper, seeded and chopped
- 1 tsp sugar

- Peel the mangoes and slice the flesh. Place into a blender or food processor with the rest of the ingredients and process until minced.
- Serve with any Indian delicacy.

Makes 1 cup

Mango & Pepper Salsa

- 2 large julie mangoes, preferably half ripe
- ½ hot pepper, seeded and chopped
- juice of 1 large lime
- ⅓ cup chopped cilantro (chadon beni)
- ¼ cup chopped chives
- ⅓ cup finely chopped bell pepper
- salt to taste
- 2 garlic cloves, minced

- Peel the mangoes and remove the flesh. Carefully cut flesh into small cubes and place in a bowl. Add the rest of the ingredients, stir and refrigerate for about 1 hour before serving.
- Serve with grilled chicken, steak or fish.

Makes about 1 cup

Pineapple & Fresh Herb Salsa

- **1 pineapple, peeled, cored and finely chopped**
- **juice of 2–3 large limes**
- **4 garlic cloves, minced**
- **⅓ cup chopped chives**
- **⅓ cup chopped cilantro (chadon beni)**
- **1 hot pepper, seeded and chopped**

- Combine all the ingredients. Refrigerate for about 1 hour before serving.
- Serve with grilled chicken breasts or fish.

Makes about 2 cups

Island Hot Sauce

This is a good regular pepper sauce. If you don't like your sauce too hot then you can remove the pepper seeds.

- **12–14 hot peppers, habaneros or scotch bonnet**
- **6 garlic cloves**
- **⅛ tsp allspice powder**
- **½ cup chopped carrots or green papaya**
- **¼ cup chopped cilantro (chadon beni)**
- **1 tsp yellow mustard**
- **½ cup white vinegar**
- **2 tsp salt**

- Remove the stems from the peppers, slice in half and remove seeds if desired.
- Place into a blender, add garlic, allspice, carrots and cilantro. Process until finely chopped. Add mustard, vinegar and salt, and process just until finely minced. Do not purée.
- Spoon into jars. The pepper sauce will keep for about 1 month.

Makes about 1 cup

Glossary of Caribbean Names and Terms

An index of Caribbean indigenous ingredients and possible substitutions.

ACCRA A fritter usually enjoyed at breakfast time made from salted cod.

ALLSPICE Also called Jamaican pimento, this is the dried berry of the pimento tree and resembles a smooth and large black peppercorn. It is a main ingredient in Jamaican jerk marinade, and is also used in pickling meats.

AREPAS A Venezuelan-inspired dish, these are little fried cornmeal pastries stuffed with a spicy meat filling.

AVOCADO A pear-shaped fruit with a thick green skin which encloses a creamy yellow flavorful pulp, delicious in soups, salads and salsas.

BAKE A flat rounded bread that is either fried or baked.

BANANA LEAVES The green leaves of the banana tree. They are usually used as a wrapping for foods to be steamed. They impart a delicate flavor to foods.

BODI A Trinidadian name for a bean much like a green bean but more than a foot long.

BREADFRUIT A round green starchy fruit on the outside, very fleshy with a pale yellow to white flesh. It is cooked and eaten as a side dish, but can be used in a variety of ways, sautéed, French fried, souffléd and grilled. Also used in savory pies and in breads.

BUSS UP SHUT The colloquial name given to paratha roti, or flaky type bread. The name derives from 'burst-up-shirt' due to the torn or ragged appearance of the bread.

CALABAZA The name given to West Indian pumpkin. This is a much denser type of pumpkin with a lower water content, and therefore much more delicious. It is also known as crapaud back pumpkin, a name reflecting its characteristic knobbly skin.

Glossary of Caribbean Names and Terms

CALLALOO A name given to the characteristic leaf of the taro/dasheen plant. It is the main ingredient in a soup with the same name, which is seasoned or cooked with ochroes, coconut milk and crab. Spinach is a suitable substitute.

CARITE A type of fresh fish resembling snapper in taste and texture.

CASSAVA An edible root vegetable from the cassava root. Also known as yuca, it is usually boiled and prepared as a vegetable.

CHADON BENI See cilantro.

CHRISTOPHENE Also known as chayote, this resembles summer squash with a rigid green skin and a pale translucent flesh. It is used as a vegetable in stir-fries, mixed vegetables and au gratin style. It is also boiled and stuffed.

CHUTNEY A very spicy condiment brought to the Caribbean by the East Indians. It is usually made with grated green mangoes or tamarind and seasoned with fresh hot peppers, cilantro and spices.

CILANTRO/CULANTRO A South American herb with the same flavor as Chinese parsley, also known as chadon beni (shadow beni) in Trinidad.

CONGO PEPPER A hot pepper species in Trinidad, also called scotch bonnet pepper in Jamaica and habanero in Mexico.

COO COO A cornmeal dish much like polenta. The Trinidadian dish is made with cornmeal, ochroes and coconut milk; the Bajan version omits the coconut milk.

DASHEEN A large root tuber, also known as taro root, the young leaves of which are used as the main ingredient in callaloo. It is very starchy and can be either purplish or white.

EDDO A root vegetable, somewhat slimy in texture, can be white or purplish in color. Very common in the Caribbean; ordinary potato may be used instead. It is related to the dasheen tuber, which is much larger and starchier in texture.

Glossary of Caribbean Names and Terms

FIGS Finger bananas.

FLAN A baked custard, very similar to crème caramel. All islands have their own version of it.

GARAM MASALA A blend of spices used in curry dishes.

GEERA Cumin.

GRANADILLA Same as passion fruit.

GROUND PROVISIONS A collective name for root vegetables, such as yams, cassavas, tannia, eddoes, dasheen, etc.

JERK Jamaican seasoning. Also a method of cooking meat that originates from Jamaica.

MELONGENE Aubergine or eggplant.

OCHRO Okra.

OIL DOWN Also known as oiled down or run down. A method of cooking root vegetables or breadfruit in coconut milk until the coconut milk is absorbed, leaving behind some coconut oil at the base of the pan.

PASSION FRUIT A highly perfumed fruit, with a thick hard inedible outer peel and a bright yellow pulp which adheres to tiny black seeds. Quite sour in taste, with a highly perfumed flavor. Excellent to use as flavoring in sorbets, ice creams and juices.

PASTELLE A popular Christmas dish in Trinidad consisting of a cornmeal dough, stuffed with a spicy meat filling, wrapped in a banana leaf and steamed.

PAW PAW An orange-fleshed fruit, filled with tiny black seeds, also known as papaya.

PIGEON PEA A rounded pea similar to the black-eyed pea.

PLANTAIN A member of the banana family. Plantains are not edible until cooked. They can be cooked at any stage, from green when they are used

Glossary of Caribbean Names and Terms

in savory dishes to very ripe when they are fried or made into desserts.

PONCHE DE CRÈME Also called poncha crème, a traditional Christmas drink, similar to eggnog, made in Trinidad and Tobago.

ROTI The outer covering of many curried foods. Much like a flour tortilla, but flavored with split peas or potato, this is used as the wrapping for curried vegetables or meat. The word 'roti' refers collectively to the wrapping with its filling.

RUN DOWN See oil down.

SALT FISH Also called salt cod. A very salty dried fish that must be soaked in water and rinsed several times before using.

SHADOW BENI A Trinidadian nickname for chadon beni. Its Spanish counterpart is culantro. The Hindus call it bandhania, meaning false dhannia.

YAM Another West Indian tuber, also called African yam, this is large, white and very starchy. Not at all like American yams, which are yellow and sweet.

YUCA Cassava.

Index

INDEX